Bighorse the Warrior

BIGHORSE
THE WARRIOR

Tiana Bighorse

Edited by Noël Bennett

Foreword by Barry Lopez

The University of Arizona Press
Tucson

The University of Arizona Press
Copyright © 1990
The Arizona Board of Regents

*Prepared by Shared Horizons with grants from The Richard C. and Susan
B. Ernst Foundation and The L. J. and Mary C. Skaggs Foundation.
All Rights Reserved*

Set in Linotron 202 Trump Mediaeval.
Manufactured in the United States of America
♾ This book is printed on acid-free, archival-quality paper.

94   93   92   91   90   5   4   3   2   1

LIBRARY OF CONGRESS CATALOGING-IN-PUBLICATION DATA
Bighorse, Tiana, 1917–
   Bighorse the warrior / Tiana Bighorse : edited by Noël Bennett
foreword by Barry Lopez.
      p.   cm.
   ISBN 0-8165-1189-6 (alk. paper)
      1. Bighorse, Gus, 1846?–1939.   2. Navajo Indians—Biography.
3. Navajo Indians—Social life and customs.   I. Bighorse, Gus,
1846?–1939.   II. Bennett, Noël, 1939–   .   III. Title.
E99.N3B5333   1990
978.9′004972—dc20   90-10874
                                                                  CIP
British Library Cataloguing in Publication data are available.

The drawings in this book are derived from ink renditions of Navajo petro-
glyphs found in Largo Canyon, New Mexico. Reproduced from *The Rocks
Begin to Speak*, by LaVan Martineau (Las Vegas, Nev.: K. C. Publications,
1973), used by permission of K. C. Publications.

Contents

Illustrations

MAPS

Foreword

In this simple story, with its vivid and sometimes heart-wrenching images of destruction, a man named Gus Bighorse speaks out of time through his daughter Tiana. What we learn of his life (1846?–1939)—a life that begins eighteen years before the descent of a Navajo nightmare called the Long Walk and ends during the Navajo stock reduction programs of the 1930s, another nightmare—arrives before us, to put it another way, in the living memory of Tiana Bighorse. It is her memory, as much as her father's recitation of evil and tribulation, that ultimately serves us.

At the heart of all literature, oral and written, we find the effort of human memory, a recapitulation of event or of feeling that binds us again to our history. The obvious surfacing of memory in narrative, the precise recall of historical event, promises at least two things: that the words in the story will flesh out the intentions and indistinct yearnings of the human heart—we will learn, again, who we are—and that the enemy, which is to forget, will be defeated.

The dramatic events of the warrior Bighorse's life, set out as they are here with no ironic reflection, without rage or self-pity, seem tragic. But his meaning, the history laid before us, is transcendent. The perpetuation of genocide he describes—a grotesque episode in North American history, routinely obscured—makes a paradox of civilization clear: the imposition of a foreign order and hierarchy on a culture does not create opportunity. It destroys coherence. It distorts personality. The loneliness of Hastiin Bighorse's early years brings into sharp focus the profound importance Navajos place on family relationships, as distinct from vaguer obligations to a national order. The fidelity of his daughter's report is an unpretentious celebration of those relationships, and a demonstration of the intrinsic value of story.

The particular life that unfolds on these pages resonates with qualities we might expect to find—anger, longing, tenderness, courage; but also, unexpectedly apparent, is wonder or awe in the face of evil. So this report by an unheard of man, through the incisive voice of his child, goes to the heart of a modern predicament—the extent to which the "reasonable" and "inevitable" destruction of traditional human relationships can be accommodated, in the name of progress or material gain, before the corrosive process undermines completely the spiritual life of a nation.

The evil we confront in modern society, which must inspire awe as well as dread and condemnation, is the way expediency triumphs so brutally over courtesy. Instead of proposing a way of life and waiting for a response, we (federal troops and administrators in this instance) impose our will and quickly silence any rejection. It is the story of colonial expansion from the Caribbean islands of the Arawak to the twentieth-century redoubts of the Montagnard.

This is a story of harm, but also of how memory in service to humanity might redeem us.

BARRY LOPEZ
McKenzie River, Oregon
February 1990

Acknowledgments

The writing of this book was sponsored by Shared Horizons through grants and contributions from

THE RICHARD C. AND SUSAN B. ERNST FOUNDATION
THE L. J. AND MARY C. SKAGGS FOUNDATION

John and Margo Ernst
Edwin L. Kennedy
Analytec Corporation

Carolyn Danley, Merton and David Gilmore, Francis Boshan, Anne and Arch Gould, Joshua and Katherine Walden, Susan McGreevy, Leora Smith, all from the United States, and Tony and Margaret Shuffrey from England.

Special assistance in the preparation of this manuscript has been received from

Automated Information Management Enterprises
  manuscript processing

David Brugge   *anthropologist, historical consultation*

John Crawford   *manuscript consultation*

Irvy W. Goossen   *Navajo language consultation*

Peter Iverson   *epigraph*

K. C. Publications   *petroglyph images*

Timothy M. Sheehan   *legal consultation*

The Museum of New Mexico Photo Archives

The Smithsonian Institution Photo Archives

Arthur Olivas, Dick Rudisill, Paula Fleming, Shawn
    Bennett, and Stephanie Koziski Olson   *photo archives
    research*

When the manuscript was complete and Shared Horizons
sought a collective wisdom to make it into a book, we sent
it to Barry Lopez. Would he contribute opening remarks?

Not long after, Barry phoned back. Yes, our instincts were
correct, it was a powerful work; yes, he would donate some remarks, would consider it an honor.

To us who have worked to make this book, Barry speaks for
us all. It has indeed been an honor.

JAMES F. WAKEMAN
Project Coordinator
Shared Horizons

Preface

I met Tiana Bighorse in 1968 in Tuba City, Arizona, on the Navajo reservation. During the next two years, she taught me spinning, dyeing, and weaving and took me into her family. I was twenty-eight and she was fifty.

Tiana learned to weave when she was seven. Her mother wove very large rugs and taught Tiana always to make a beautiful rug and never to let Navajo weaving be forgotten. So in 1971 Tiana and I made a book, *Working with the Wool: How To Weave a Navajo Rug.* We made it for Navajo girls to keep close to their traditions. We made it for the general public to appreciate the beauty of the Navajo weaving process. It was a legacy—Tiana's mother's stories.

"How about my father's stories?" I had moved to Shonto, a more remote part of the reservation, and Tiana wrote me there. I thought back on our time together in Tuba City. I didn't remember her telling me much about her father. Nothing of his stories. Had she waited until my weaving tutelage was complete? Had I been too immersed in the loom to remember? I saw her several times in the next few months, but she never mentioned her father, and at the end of the year I moved again. The stories were still untold.

Constant letters between us shared family news and the world of color and design we wove on our loom. Tiana again brought up the stories, suggesting we make another book. But I could see no clear way. We lived four hours apart. I had a family—a young child accustomed to closeness, a physician husband accustomed to order, a small house with no guest room. But a sensitive writer friend lived in Flagstaff, Arizona, just an hour south of Tuba City. Maybe they could collaborate. I set up a first meeting between them.

"I liked your friend," Tiana wrote me later, "but no stories came out."

In 1973 Tiana wrote me, "I'm here in Spokane visiting Leonard's wife. The kids go to school all day long and it's lonely here."

"How about your father's stories? You could write them down."

"My English isn't good; nobody'd understand me. I don't spell right."

"That doesn't matter. Just write them down. Every time you think of a story, write it down so it won't be forgotten. Later, maybe your kids can help you make a book. Or when I can, I will."

In the following years there were more letters and more visits; I had another child, divorced, moved, wrote more books about Navajo weaving, organized national conferences on southwestern textiles. Then in 1986, when I was visiting Tiana on reservation, she pulled some papers out of a top dresser drawer and laid them beside me on the couch—a stack of ruled binder papers an inch high.

"Do you want to see these?"

I glanced at the top page, thumbed through the pile. Scrambled cursive filled the hand-worn sheets.

"What are they?"

"My father's stories."

My God, I thought, *she's been writing those stories all these years!* I could scarcely make sense of the irregular scrawl, sometimes penciled between uniform blue lines, sometimes scrunched into margins. I was confused. The papers seemed to have been shuffled—passed through various hands, dropped, reassembled without order. The same stories appeared in different places, sometimes full and complete, sometimes segmented, fractionated. In the long twelve-year span, had she forgotten she'd written them before?

I reminded myself Tiana was translating from Navajo into English and that Navajo has no equivalent tenses. Long ago I'd become accustomed to hearing English-speaking Navajos shift between past, present, and future—in the same paragraph, in the same sentence. Now these same tense changes on the written page were strangely disorienting.

But I was intent on finding meaning beyond the form, so I read on, collecting clues. Running, hiding, bands of warriors, Canyon de Chelly, Kit Carson—suddenly it was clear. Tiana was writing about the Long Walk!

I had always considered the Long Walk a tragic low point in history. America, the land of the free and the brave, dedicated to the ideals of human equality. The U.S. cavalry, relentlessly hunting down, subduing, ousting indigenous people from their land. White marauders, using threats of death, herding their fellow man some three hundred miles on foot. Imprisoning a race for four long, disease-filled years. Decimating a tribe.

Traditionally, the conqueror writes his own history, etches for posterity the noble vision, overlooks the brutality that brought it into being. So American history texts forget to tabulate that about nine thousand Navajos began the forced march. And half never returned—old people, pregnant women, children who couldn't keep up.

But now a humane story could be told from the Navajo point of view. It was a story of disease, starvation, brutality. Equally important, it was a story of human triumph: the vision and compassion of the Navajo leaders; the courage of the warriors; the endurance of the people themselves. And through it all ran an unmistakably deep and compelling love for the Land.

"I didn't know your father led bands of warriors under Chief Manuelito. You mean, those were some of the men Kit Carson never got?"

My friend nodded. I held the papers close. "When do we start?"

My home in Corrales, New Mexico, had the advantage of a word processor, but it was an eight-hour drive from Tuba City. Tiana hadn't been off the reservation much. Besides the prob-

Tiana Bighorse

lem of transportation, I was concerned for her comfort in strange places. So we worked it out: her son, Billy, would drive her halfway; I would meet them in Gallup, bring her home.

Driving through the Red Rocks near Fort Wingate, we began envisioning the book. We each brought up questions we had, and our hopes. My foremost thought was to protect the integrity of the Navajo voice; these would be *her* words and thoughts, not mine. Through the town of Grants and past the Pueblo of Laguna, Tiana wondered who would be telling the stories, she or her father? Eventually she decided it would be her father, and moreover, he would tell the stories in the present tense because it's closest to how he told them. "He always makes it feel like it's happening right now."

Then there was the question of context. Since Navajo oral history is devoid of specific dates, should I provide a linear, historical framework for non-Navajo readers? If so, how? Footnotes on dates and related U.S. history seemed disruptive to the "as told" sense of the Navajo stories. More disturbing was their implication that the text was invalid unless annotated by an Anglo sense of history. I decided to add an historical context in which events in Gus Bighorse's life would be referenced to significant events in U.S. history.

The next morning I sat at the word processor.

"Okay, let's begin. You tell me the first story. I'll write down just what you say."

"I can't talk to that machine!"

"It's okay. You can talk to *me*. *I'll* talk to the machine."

She looked directly at me, eyes fixed on avoiding the monitor, then looked away. I waited. No words came.

I tried to remember Navajo protocol. I was beginning to sense how important a twenty-year friendship and eight years of living on reservation were going to be to this book.

"Well, . . . just to get started, . . . I'll pretend I'm you. I'll tell those people out there who I am and how I know these stories." I got myself in the mood. "Let's see, I'm Navajo, so I don't start with my name—I start with my clan?"

She nodded.

I typed into the word processor, "I'm a Navajo of the Bįįh Bitoodnii Clan. I started to weave when I was seven—"

"No, you don't say that yet!"

"Oh. What do I say?"

"I'm a Navajo of the Bįįh Bitoodnii Clan. My name is Tiana Bighorse. I am seventy-one years old. My hometown is Tuba City, Arizona. I started to weave when I was seven—"

"Wait! Slow down, I can't type that fast."

But it was too late. The stories that had waited fifty years to be recorded were coming out.

"How was it?" I picked Tiana up at the Albuquerque Greyhound bus depot. It had been several months since our initial work week. First she couldn't get a ride to Gallup, and my driving to Tuba City to bring her and take her back again would cost us four writing days. I was hesitant to suggest she ride the bus, which she had never done by herself. Being alone among strangers is scary, especially to the large-familied Navajo, where eleven people live easily in a hogan and five consistently fill the front seat of a pickup. But today, past the age of seventy, Tiana had undertaken her first solo trip.

"How was it?"

"Well, it's okay. You know, I get in that bus in Flagstaff and there are lots of Navajos in there. And the bus stops lots of times when it's coming here, and every time those Navajos get off. Well, when it stops at Winslow, lots of Navajos get off. Then it stops at Holbrook. And I'm the only one still sitting there. There's other people sitting there, but no one dressed like me—blouse, velvet, and all this turquoise. And it goes again, and after a while a young Navajo guy comes over to me. He is polite, and he talks to me in Navajo.

"'My grandmother, maybe you miss your stop. Maybe you are supposed to get off in Holbrook.' He just talks to me like this. He thinks I'm making a mistake, I'm too old to be riding past the reservation by myself."

Tiana looked around, keeping track of the depot activity. In Flagstaff her belongings had routinely been checked through to Albuquerque. Now the bus driver was unloading the baggage compartment and Tiana was watching each suitcase and parcel, anxious about her clothes and other belongings tied up in a Pendleton blanket.

"I guess he's worried about me, why I'm on the bus, just me by myself. That's why he's talking to me like that, that young man on the bus, talking to me in Navajo. So I just look right at him and I say to him in my best English, 'No, I didn't miss my stop. I'm supposed to be right here. I'm going to Albuquerque, New Mexico!'"

I laughed, enjoying the Navajo humor and glad to be with her again. I picked up her bundle and started for the car. "Maybe you should have told him you're going to Albuquerque, New Mexico, to write *another* book," I teased. She looked at me quizzically. Within the traditional way, blatantly stating one's own accomplishments constitutes something more than bad taste. But she suddenly smiled. Tentatively, then broadly. She was in Albuquerque, New Mexico, willing to relax into Anglo cultural humor and certainly ready to write another book.

For me, making a book means long days at the word processor—writing, editing, revising. I wondered how this process would be for Tiana, who'd never done it before. As it turned out, each morning when I got up she was already downstairs, reading what we'd written the day before, thinking of ways to make it clearer, adding details she forgot to include. At breakfast we'd talk about what she'd tell me next, and then we'd get to work. At about three o'clock we'd look up, surprised it was so late, and make ourselves lunch. More writing, then dinner near eight, and after that—agreeing we were tired and would only edit—we'd end up writing far into the night. She was determined to tell her story.

In the process, our table became strewn with maps of the Southwest, her penciled papers, Navajo dictionaries. When she came to a word she didn't know in English, she used Navajo. Sometimes I understood. If not, I searched for it in a dictionary, tracked down a written equivalent of her complex sounds, inflections, glottal stops. I was calling hard on my two semesters of Navajo language and the vocabulary Tiana had taught me. Had all my reservation culture and language lessons been for this very purpose?

Often as I typed I wondered how she could remember so many details. Her clarity seemed absolute. Unfaltering. I knew that accuracy of memory is different in the Navajo culture than in the Anglo. But I was seeing it now in action.

Years ago I learned that Father Berard Haile first wrote in the Navajo language in 1910. It amused me that Navajo was written by Anglos, for Anglos. Later, I saw its uselessness to the traditional people, who simply, clearly, and accurately re-membered things, then passed them along by word of mouth. One time Tiana watched me write down page after page of a complicated two-face/twill weaving pattern. After a while she told me, "Just keep it in your head. Only when you know things that way are they yours. That way they're there when you want them and nobody can ever take them away from you." She didn't understand, she said, the Anglo brain on pa-per. Keeping complex details in mind became more real the longer I stayed on reservation, where memory is essential for survival. Eventually I understood why the old people exhorted the young to pay attention. Watch. Listen.

I heard one grandfather admonish his grandson while teach-ing him the constellations. "I'm going to show you once. I want you to remember for the rest of your life. And if you ever forget, you'll go blind." Now Tiana was effortlessly retelling the stories her father had told her fifty years before.

I wondered, too, how it happened, in a culture that clearly classifies and separates the ownership of male and female sto-ries, that a young Navajo girl had become privy to men's sto-ries. I asked Tiana about it. She said her father told his stories of what it meant to be a warrior late at night to men around the fire, and to her brothers when Tiana was in bed "asleep." But her brothers caught her listening and told their father to make her stop. Her father reprimanded her, told her these were men's stories, for men alone to hear. And Tiana pretended to go to sleep.

One day young Tiana asked her father a question about a detail of the stories, and her father realized she had been listening all along—the only one really listening. The only one remembering. After that, when her brothers said, "Make her stop listening!" the father reprimanded them. Tiana was going to be the one to pass the stories to the next generation.

And here we were now, she and I, sitting together, telling age-old stories to a word processor. In this ironic way we were fulfilling a long-nurtured mandate. I thought back on the fifty-year-old Tiana, whom I met in 1968 when I first came to her hogan, asking her to teach me to weave. I recalled in her visage a certain hesitancy, as though evaluating something. In the years since, I've wondered what she saw in that critical moment, for her look softened.

"How long do you have?"

"Two years," I replied evenly, confidently. Then, seeing again a slight tightening of her brow, I added, "Will that be enough?"

Now, within that fifty-year-old Tiana standing at the hogan, I saw a young girl holding tightly somehow to promises made long ago. Maybe it was young Tiana, at that moment, who intuitively saw in me a way to fulfill them. It was young Tiana who said yes.

When the manuscript was complete, I sent it to the University of Arizona Press, which in turn gave it to a scholarly reader for preliminary comment. In time the remarks came back. The reader wrote that the stories "illustrate many of the ideals and values of traditional Navajo people and, in their spare straightforwardness, eloquently represent Navajo ways of thinking and expressing thoughts." But from there the reader called attention to their "problematical language style," stating that "bad English grammar should not represent intelligent thought." She pointed out that the author probably speaks grammatically perfect Navajo, so we should edit out her errors in English to reveal her "true voice."

Tiana and I had stumbled into a full-blown scholarly debate: Should "Red English" be employed as a standard literary form?

I brought Tiana's stories up on my word processor. "I got seven children," the monitor said.

"Never say got," my high school English teacher reprimanded. "I *had* seven children," I began to type.

Whitewash! an inner voice interrupted. *You're arbitrarily changing words. Not for clarity now, but to fit some conventionalized scholarly Anglo form. There'll be no stopping till it's grammatically perfect. Then where's the storyteller? Her personality? Cultural nuance?*

Editing was precarious. It reminded me of the first time I restored an historic Navajo blanket. Twenty years ago a dealer brought me a hundred-year-old serape. Would I reweave it? I was wary. Reweaving meant taking out some of the old yarn and putting in new—sheer folly in a rare fabric of cochineal yarn. Yet gaping holes despoiled its beauty.

"We'll go slow, preserve the age, maybe just fill in the major holes. Nothing irreversible. Nothing that can't be undone if better methods or philosophies evolve."

The trader agreed and I began. I precisely matched size, spin, and colors of yarn and then painstakingly rewove the discontinuous designs with their subtle color shifts. But when the dealer came to pick it up, he was upset. The major holes were completely gone, and the minor ones stood out. I reluctantly agreed to reweave these as well. But then small holes were disruptive—including moth damage I'd never seen before. In the end, after I'd reworked everything down to the frayed selvage cords, the owner took home a perfect textile, happy. But to me it looked brand-new; the serape's historic integrity was gone. And I had done it.

Now I faced the manuscript.

I had started with a clear purpose: to protect the integrity of the Navajo voice. Then, for reader clarity, I had standardized most verbs in present tense, edited them to agree with their subject, and corrected disorienting words—such as *man* when Tiana meant men. I had rewoven the large and middle-sized holes.

"I got seven children," the monitor said. *A small discontinuity in form,* my inner voice insisted. *A mere frayed edge in a timeless tapestry.*

Restoration lessons hadn't stopped with the serape. Years further into my reweaving career, I'd become interested in the wear patterns of old textiles. Stretched sections told how a fabric had been worn. Raveled ends showed where a blanket had been held tightly closed. Thin areas implied repeated leaning—perhaps against the trading post or hogan wall. But blankets that had been restored down to their thin warp and frayed edges showed nothing. Pertinent cultural information, lost forever because the restorer didn't distinguish damage from wear, didn't know what to weave and what to leave, didn't know when to stop.

Now I wanted to preserve the storyteller's essence in this culturally rich manuscript. Now I needed to distinguish perspicuity from formality. So I reread Tiana's stories. They were clear and very Navajo. I switched the monitor off; my part was done.

In Navajo Way, Tiana's stories are a vessel of culture. They gift a specific segment of the tribe—the young male generation—with a sense of their heritage. These are, as her brothers knew and guarded, men's stories. A sacred part of the Male Way. It is important that the message comes in story form, for the story is a source of power. "It's important to the Navajos when you know these kind of stories. They can keep you going. These are brave stories, and knowing them can make you brave," Tiana tells us in her introduction.

The underlying theme of the stories is what it is to be a warrior. The Bighorse manuscript offers a more profound view than the Hollywood stereotype of pinto ponies and wanton scalping. Once, after a long week of writing in Corrales, Tiana wrote me again from Tuba City. She was determined that I understand what *warrior* means in Navajo:

> When Mr. Bighorse is a boy, he goes with his father. His father teaches everything that a boy should do to become a man. And what he shouldn't do. And his father tells him, "You will be brave and be a warrior someday."
>
> In Navajo, a warrior means someone who can get through the snowstorm when no one else can.
>
> In Navajo, a warrior is the one that doesn't get the flu when everyone else does—the only one walking around, making a fire for the sick, giving them medicine, feeding them food, making them strong to fight the flu.
>
> In Navajo, a warrior is the one who can use words so everyone knows they are part of the same family.
>
> In Navajo, a warrior says what is in the people's hearts. Talks about what the land means to them. Brings them together to fight for it.

So Tiana brings new meaning to the word *warrior*. Her father's stories translate the term exquisitely as *vision, compassion, courage,* and *endurance.* So does Tiana by her actions. In making this book, I've seen her call on each of these qualities, watched her step well beyond her traditional culture to gift Life back to the tribe—and to the world. Tiana, then, is a female embodiment of the warrior. And we are grateful. For in this very act she amplifies the vision one more time. She calls to the warrior within us all.

NOËL BENNETT
January 1989

Introduction

I am a Navajo of the Bįįh Bitoodnii (Deer Spring) Clan. My name is Tiana Bighorse. I am seventy-one years old. My home-town is Tuba City, Arizona.

I started to weave when I was seven, and when I was eight I went to school. I went up to the ninth grade in the Tuba City Boarding School. Then my mother got sick. I'm her only daughter, and I got three brothers. There was nobody else to take care of her. I just quit school to take care of her. Good thing I did. She lived just a few more years. I was twenty-one when my father died and twenty-two when my mother died.

After my parents died, a year and a half later I met a man and we got married. I was twenty-three years old. His name was Fred Butler, Jr. But there were no jobs where we were, so we had to go to Utah to support ourselves. We worked on the sugar beets. While we worked on hoeing the sugar beet fields, I still wove rugs in between the work. I always weave wher-ever I go.

Now I got seven children. When I was raising them, I didn't have a regular job, I just wove. I bought food and clothes for them. My weaving always supports us. Weaving comes from our ancestors. To the Navajo it's very important to hold onto weaving and the Navajo culture. That way it won't be forgotten.

I promised my mom I would never set aside what a great culture she taught me, and so in 1971 I made a book about weaving. The name of the book is *Working with the Wool*. It's a great book for the young generation. They are using the book to teach children in boarding school and even college students.

My father's name was Bighorse. He was of the Tsé Deesh-gizhnii [Rock Gap] Clan, and his father was Tábąąhá (Edge-water) Clan. They called him Asdzą́ą́ Łį́į́' Yiishchį́įh Biyáázh—Son-of-the-Woman-Who-Is-Expert-with-Horses.

When I was small I just listened to my father's stories. I am really interested in them, and what he is telling. Sometimes he is just telling stories and nobody else is listening—I'm the only one sitting there and listening to him. Sometimes he is telling lots of men what it is to be a warrior. Sometimes he is telling us when we are by ourselves, just talking to my brothers while I'm lying in bed. They don't want me to listen because it's just the men that are supposed to be listening. They think about it that way. They don't like it when I'm listening, so my brothers say, "She's not supposed to be listening. Make her stop." So my father says not to listen. He tells me the stories are not for me to hear. So I just pretend I'm asleep. But after a while, my father finds out. He finds out I'm the only one who is really listening. The only one who is remembering the stories. So after a while, when my brothers say, "Make her stop listening!" my father says, "It's okay, let her listen. She knows two languages, Navajo and English, so maybe it's good that she's listening, and maybe someday you will have forgotten and have to ask her, and she can tell you. She's a girl, and if she has kids, then she'll tell them stories she heard from me. They will be told to my great-grandkids." That's what he said.

The stories my father tells us, they are scary stories—how the cavalry was there and how everyone gets killed, and how the kids and the ladies get killed.

The way my father tells the stories, it's like it's happening right there. That's how I don't forget it. I remember. It makes me think what a brave man he was, and all the other warriors, how brave they all were. And what good leaders we had—Manuelito and all the chiefs. They give the warriors and their people courage to stand on their feet and not give up.

My father fought for the Navajo land with hundreds and hundreds of Navajo warriors, with bows and arrows. And lots of Navajos did their job. And now what he said is right. I ask my two older brothers about our father's stories, but they don't remember any.

I love my father. Maybe that's why he gave me all that
memory of the stories he told. Maybe that's why it's in my
mind all this time. It's in my heart and in my living. It's important to the Navajos when you know these kind of stories.
They can keep you going. These are brave stories, and knowing
them can make you brave.

I don't want to just throw away what he told us. Right now
the young generation knows nothing. They don't know stories
about anything. They just think that this is our land and it
was given to us by the Great Spirit. But their great-grand-
ancestors didn't tell them. The reservation was fought for.

I decided to write another book. I want the people to know
the warriors are brave to fight with the enemies. I want the
world to know that the Navajo warriors were heros. They fight
against the cavalries. Lots of Navajos shed blood. I make this
book for the young generation to read and know the courage of
the Navajo warriors, what our ancestors did for us. They fight
for what they believe in. They suffer hardship at Fort Sumner.
They pay for our land with their lives.

I want everyone to remember how the Navajo got this big
reservation. They will tell their grandchildren, and our warriors will not be forgotten.

Bighorse the Warrior

To the Navajo, the Long Walk happened last week.

—PETER IVERSON

Once the Navajo lived on their own land. They believed that the Great Spirit put them on that land to live there and to die of old age there. The land fed them and their children and their sheep and horses. The rain was plentiful and nourished their crops. The sun brought warmth and its blessing to life. They prayed to their Father Sky and Mother Earth. The land and all of nature were everything to them.

In the 1860s the Navajo were taken from the land they loved by the United States government. They were forced to walk three hundred miles and then imprisoned, starved, and badly treated. Thousands lost their lives. Those who were not captured, who successfully hid from Kit Carson and the cavalry, lived in constant fear.

The Navajo men and women who survived the Long Walk and the following years of impoverishment are now dead. But their story lives in the collective memory of the tribe.

Why I Tell My Stories

I want to tell my life story. My name is
Gus Bighorse, and I am Tsé Deeshgizhnii [Rock Gap] Clan. And my father's
clan is Tábąąhá [Edgewater] Clan.

I was born near Mount Taylor around
1846. I'm the only child in the family.

I am old now. Some days when I am herding sheep I can't
see too well 'cause it looks like it's foggy. I just say I'm not
ready yet. My time is coming, but it's okay. Someday it will be
the end of my journey, but I've had a long life, and I will live
through my children and my grandchildren and my great-
grandchildren and even three times great-grandchildren. And
I am happy and I love every one of them.

I have survived wars and many hardships. I never thought of
going this far. And I am thankful for all my clan children. I'm
not going to let my grandchildren suffer what I suffered. I suffered *for* them.

I survived the great war of Navajo and cavalry. And after the
peace came, that's when I got married and got these kids. On
top of it, my first wife died and I got only the kids. And the
next wife was her sister, and I got more kids, and I think how
I can support my children. They were small when their
mother died, and I have to take care of them. And I plant corn
and watermelon and raise horses and sheep, and that's how I
have to take care of them. And the farming was really good for
me to support my children. And that time there was rain, and
it was really plentiful for my livestock and my crops. That's
how I raised my kids, and that's how I really did my job on this
earth. I'm thankful for the guidance I have, and for this long
life that I have.

2

There will be war again someday. There won't be peace all the way. The white people were going to take the land away from us, but we fought for it and kept part of our own land.

Or maybe not war. Maybe someday the white people will give you something you like that will be getting rid of you. This is an old Navajo word they always say, *bááhádzid*, danger. It means you think it's harmless, but you have to be careful. Something will sting you, like a scorpion or an ant. But don't try to bother with it. Don't try to touch it. It's just the same as an enemy. It kills people.

I always say, life will not be easy. But, bad as it is, we Navajos know we were the least unfortunate of all the western Indians. We started our living again, we struggled to survive. And the only thing in the world we have is our own life and the land we want to keep to live on.

Nowadays the men and the boys should be thinking about how they could survive like I survived. It must be in your thinking and in your life to be brave and to be safe.

My Parents' Background

My mother was Tsé Deeshgizhnii [Rock Gap] Clan. She had been trained to hunt, and she could run like a horse. And she could weave her own dress. That means she just made one *biil* [traditional dress] for half a year. It was woven with cotton and wool. And she could do silversmithing, too.

My father was Tábąąhá Clan. That means Edgewater. He knew how to make saddles and bridles for the horses. He was a good hunter, and he made bows and arrows, really strong ones. He was a brave man, too. He fought against the Mexicans and chased them back to their land. That's where my father got his horses.

My father said, "A man should be right to stand up straight for what he believes." I always keep it in mind. Because my father thinks I will be a man someday, he says, "The sky is our father and the earth is our mother. If you get in trouble with the enemy, always look up to your Father Sky. You are already in your Mother Earth's hand."

My father takes me all over the Navajo land to see the place when I am nine years old. We ride mostly every day—four years, summer and winter. We always start from Tsoodził, Mount Taylor, where we live and keep coming back. Mount Taylor is the sacred mountain of the South. We go to Leupp and to Flagstaff. We go around Dook'o'oosłííd, San Francisco Peaks, a sacred mountain of the West. And from there to Grand Canyon, and around Lee's Ferry and around Navajo Mountain and through Four Corners. And around the sacred

The Navajo hogan of mud over a log framework provides a well-insulated living structure in a hot desert land. Here a silversmith and his family display the tools of the craft—hammer and anvil, bellows, and bow drill.

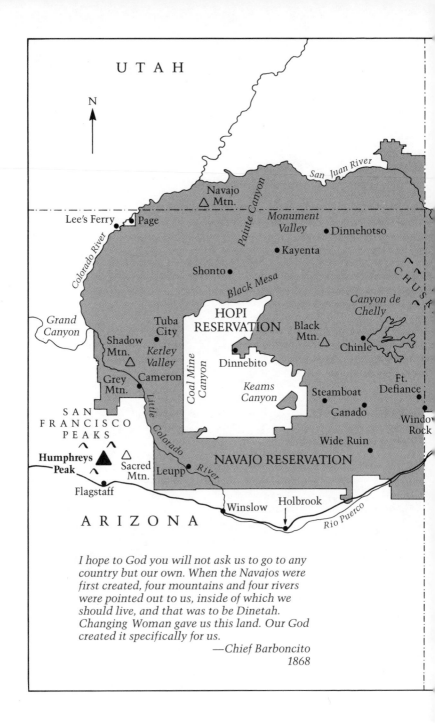

I hope to God you will not ask us to go to any
country but our own. When the Navajos were
first created, four mountains and four rivers
were pointed out to us, inside of which we
should live, and that was to be Dinetah.
Changing Woman gave us this land. Our God
created it specifically for us.

—Chief Barboncito
1868

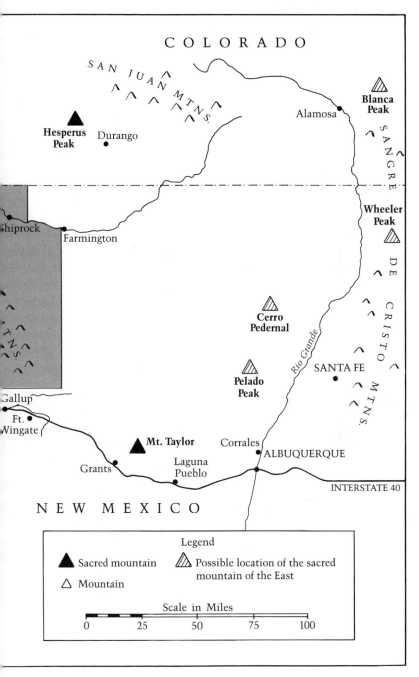

COLORADO

SAN JUAN MTNS.

Hesperus Peak

Durango

Alamosa

Blanca Peak

SANGRE

Wheeler Peak

hiprock   Farmington

DE

Cerro Pedernal

Rio Grande

CRISTO

Pelado Peak

SANTA FE

Gallup

Ft. Wingate

TNS.

Mt. Taylor   Corrales

ALBUQUERQUE

Grants   Laguna Pueblo

INTERSTATE 40

N E W   M E X I C O

Legend

▲ Sacred mountain

△ Mountain

⬗ Possible location of the sacred
  mountain of the East

Scale in Miles

0   25   50   75   100

Map 1. Lands of the Navajo

mountain of the North, Big Sheep Mountain, Dib'e Ntsaa.[1] We even get near Sisnaajiní,[2] the sacred mountain of the East. And then to Shiprock and Farmington, Chinle, and Gallup. We go all the way to Albuquerque to visit some pueblo friends, and to Santa Fe. We see some white Americans at Santa Fe, and they are friends to the Indians. We always go back to Mount Taylor.

I am always surprised that I see Navajos in this land wherever we go. There are no white Americans on the Navajo land. The Navajos live in peace.

We want to know how big the Navajo land is, and we find out. It is big. I can't believe it. Some places we stop and stay there for two days to let our horses rest. While we are there we run about four miles a day on foot to see where water is. Every place we find water holes there is always somebody living there, or a little place with corn or watermelon.

There are lots of places that have real rich soil to plant, and some places it is rocky. And some places you can find lots of cedar trees and pine trees and piñon nut trees. The scene I will never forget is Monument Valley. It is a place you can't believe how it came to be put there. It looks like somebody was just playing and stood up the rocks so they will be beautiful to see. I think the Great Spirit put them there for us. I never dream that is where I will play hide and seek with the enemy.

I am very happy my father takes me everywhere to look at all these places. By the time I am fifteen years old, I am already taught to be a brave warrior.

1. Hesperus Peak, San Juan Mountains, Colorado.
2. Sisnaajiní translates as The-Mountain-That-Is-Black-Belted. But there is dispute among Navajo medicine men and among Anglo scholars regarding which mountain is the sacred mountain of the East. The four possibilities are Blanca Peak in Colorado; Wheeler Peak near Taos, New Mexico; Cerro Pedernal near Abiquiu, New Mexico; and Pelado Peak north of Jemez Pueblo, New Mexico.

Growing Up

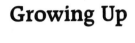

When a Navajo meets a
Navajo, the first thing
asked is, What clan are
you? That is the way the re-
lationship goes. There are all
different clans. Some of them
are related. If you're related, you
can call each other Father or Cousin or Grandpa or Grandma
or Brother or Sister or Uncle. When you meet someone, you
don't say, "Hi, my name is ———." Instead you say, "I come
from this place," and you tell them your clan. And they will
say, "I'm the same clan," or, "My father's the same clan." And
then you call them by how they are related to you, not by their
name.

My father knows lots of people all over the reservation. We
go mostly in the summertime to visit. I know all the names of
the places, and I know how far it is to go over to each place.

My father talks with his relatives about how they can share
the field to plant. They sit up and talk all night. I keep myself
awake to hear what they are talking about. They tell stories
about how we came to this world, and how the clans started
separating. They have lots to tell. And how you could be a
good hunter, and how you could make a hogan and take care of
horses. You have to take care of your horses and keep them fat
and healthy so you can go a long way without any trouble. My
father used to tell me how to take good care of the horses. If
you have three or four horses, you don't ride one horse all the
way. You have to have an extra one to take turns to ride. And
about being a good hunter. You can use the head and skin of

the deer to disguise yourself. That way you can get near to the deer to kill it.

I think the most wonderful place the Navajo have is Many Farms, and Farmington too. I think, if I ever get married, I will live in Farmington. That is the place I pick out when I am twelve years old. I think my father will be with me all my life and that he will find a girl for me around that area. I realize later I am wrong. Instead, my father gets killed there, and I have to think about that place all my life.

We often go to Farmington in the summer. There is lots of corn. It grows about six feet tall. There are lots of watermelon, pumpkins too, and cantaloupe and apples and peaches. My father has clan relatives that live there. Whenever it is time for us to go, they pack our horses with lots of goodies. We pack four horses, but we still don't get everything on the horse.

We go over there every summer, and sometimes my mom goes with us. When the corn is ready to eat, my mother helps make a "kneel-down bread." She grinds the fresh corn, and they use corn husks, and they roll the corn in them and put them in the ground to cook. And when they take them out, they just chop them up and put them in the sun to dry. Then they can save them for the winter.

And they fix the corn another way to use in the winter. They cook corn on the cob, cook them on the charcoal. And they dry them and use them for winter too. They boil them when they need them. They cook lots of them and cut them and put them in the sun to dry. And they fix the peaches the same way. They dry all these for winter food.

My father already taught me how to plant. We help our clan relatives plant watermelon and corn and cantaloupe. There is water for irrigation, and the crops are really good.

When I am sixteen years old, we live near Mount Taylor. One day I go to the mountain to hunt for food—rabbits, berries, wild potatoes, and there are wild onions too. My parents are busy at home. In the afternoon I return with the food. I find my parents laying there. It looks like they've been murdered by someone that came along. I see horse tracks around and some blood on the horse track. It looks like they tried to shoot back with bows and arrows. I think they wounded or killed two. It looks like those guys took the wounded back on the horse.

So I just sit down and think about what a terrible thing happened, and why it happened, and who did it. I just sit down for a long time and think about it. And everything is still there that they were working on, like silver that my mother was working on, and the saddle and bridle my father was making. Those things are all there. The killers didn't rob them.

So I just think about burying them. I start to dig right there, and I'm in a great sorrow. I just bury both of them with all their work. The saddle and everything I bury with them. I'm just really upset about all these things. I had never thought of losing both parents at the same time.

And I sit down and think about it, and why and how it happened. If I had been here, I would have been killed too. It's a good thing I took off. That way I didn't get killed. But maybe if I stayed with my parents, maybe they wouldn't get killed. I wish I could have saved them. And I think to myself, This is the way it is when they say you're poor. I think to myself, Now I'm poor. Now I understand what it is to be poor. Nobody had ever talked to me about this, so I just have to think about it myself. If somebody don't have nothing, that don't mean they're poor. If you lose both your mom and dad, *that* means you're poor.

So I pick up the leftover arrows and the bows, and I think where to go. I just leave from there and go to the mountain to see if I can survive somewhere. I think, As long as I can stand on my two feet, I can keep going forward, and if I survive, someday maybe I will be happy again and tell the stories of

Manuelito was one of the preeminent Navajo chiefs. He directed the warriors in their strategic maneuvers to resist round-up by the U.S. cavalry.

what happened in the past and what hardship I went through.
So I just leave for the mountain to meet somebody to tell me
what's going on.

When I get to the mountain I hear some talking way up in
the woods. I go up there. It's the Navajos. I'm really surprised.
What had happened to me was what had happened to them.
They had lost their mothers or their aunts or their relatives
and come up here too.

And there's some warriors already here. They have news
that the enemy is coming. The enemy is some soldiers from
Washington. They want to get our land. That's why they're
killing all these Navajos. They tell me the soldiers chopped all
the corn and peaches down and burned them. They tell me
that my father's relatives got killed trying to stop them—
protecting the corn and peaches.

I got nobody to tell what happened to my parents. The relatives of my father don't know about my parents' death. They,
too, got killed. I got no relatives to go to. It is really heartache.
How I loved that place, and how the crops grew. I had always
been willing to help plant. Somebody don't have any love to
destroy the crops and to burn the Mother Earth.

I am thinking about my parents mostly. I really don't want
to fight. But I'm thinking that I have to fight for my land and
my parents and myself. I don't want the enemy to capture me
or kill me. I don't want to die in a prison. I think to myself,
I want to be a brave warrior like my father taught me.

And pretty soon lots of more men are coming up the mountain. Some are elderly men and some are old men. They talk to
me like my father. They tell me to be brave. It's hard for me
to think about killing. But there is a chief. His name is Ch'il
Haajíní. They call him Manuelito. He tells us to fight for our
land. He really cares about his own people. He wants them all
safe. He wants them to be in their own land. Soon I feel like
fighting along with them, and that's what we did finally. We
started. It's hard to do, but we did it.

Somebody told us more cavalries will be coming and more killing going on. Instead of waiting to get killed, we start to make bows and arrows, and pretty soon we are joining bands to fight.

The bows and arrows are hard to make. You have to use special bushes for the arrow—straight ones and all the same length. You have to cut a whole bunch of them and put them in the wet sand. And the next day you have to straighten it and use a rock and sand it down. Then when it is still wet, you have to use your teeth. Chew it to toughen it, the whole thing up to the end. This bush that makes the arrow is called *tsitł'iz*, hard wood.[3]

And you have to have an eagle feather—one feather for each arrow. And you split the feather and use the tree gum to make it stick. And you make an arrowhead with some kind of metal. Then you put designs on the stick. On one side you put a lightning with four zigzag points. This is for the enemy to be shot. On the other side you just make a straight line going through. This is for the warrior. It's like a safe path. At the base, right next to the feather, you put four stripes, each one a different color: white, blue, yellow, black. They're for the warrior too—safety from all directions. Next you put mountain lion fat or bear fat on the arrow. This is to poison the person you shoot.

And the bow is made of oak tree. You have to straighten it out, clear all the branches off to make it smooth, then put it in the ground, and when it is still wet, curve it to make a bow. Then sand it with a rock. The oak holds the curve real good. That's why we use it. It has to be tough to shoot real far. And we make a little gap at the top to hold the bowstring. We use horsehide or cowhide or deerhide to make the bowstring. Horsehide is the one that is really tough. It makes a bow string that don't break.

3. Fendler Bush.

And you have to wear the bow guard. If you're not wearing it, you will hurt your hand shooting. That's why all the men always have one on their wrist. Any kind of hide is good for that. Also, to carry the arrows you have to make a quiver, so when you start shooting you can just pull the arrows out fast. The arrows are not heavy; you carry thirty or forty. Your fingers and arms have to be strong too. We all have to make ourselves strong to stand with our bows and arrows against the enemy's guns.

The older men teach the young boys to make bows and arrows—to hunt for oak trees and hard, tough bushes in the mountains, to hunt the animals for the hides. And we put bands of warriors on the highest peak or mesa or mountain so they can see the enemy come through.

After the cavalry chop and burn down the crops, the soldiers go to the Navajo hogans. They tell the families to go to Tséhootsooí, Fort Defiance, to get their free food. That's how they gather all the people at Fort Defiance. But some of the families hide, and some are found by the cavalry and are killed right there. Sometimes just the man is killed trying to protect the family, and the cavalry takes the family and the sheep over there to the fort.

The warriors don't want to go to Fort Defiance. They just stay in the mountains and fight for their land.

Fort Defiance was built by the white soldiers. The soldiers just stay inside the fort, and the horses are outside. No fence around it. The soldiers have lots of horses, and they order us Navajos to keep our horses away from their pastureland. Manuelito is very angry about this because there is no fence around the pasture. It is really hard to keep our horses away from there.

One morning some soldiers ride out of the fort and shoot all our horses in the pastureland. Our chief gets real mad. We love our horses more than anything, you know. These are our only tame horses. The soldiers had already shot other wild horses

Prior to the Long Walk, Navajos who surrendered or were captured were held at Fort Defiance, a garrison laid out with white man's symmetry in the natural Southwest setting.

around the water hole, but these were our trained horses. We used them almost every day.

Manuelito tells us to round up the horses that belong to the white soldiers. So we go over there to capture a few horses. We think we are going to take just their horses in exchange for what they shot of ours. But the white soldiers start shooting at us. They have their guns. We have only bows and arrows and old Mexican guns. We shoot at each other, and some Navajos get killed, and some white soldiers get killed. We take off again and go to our hiding place after this happens.

We are there for nearly three weeks when a messenger runner tells us there are more soldiers coming into the fort. Manuelito knew that was what they were going to do—send to Washington for some more soldiers. They start attacking us and other small bands of warriors, so we gather more warriors in the mountains.

By next February there are lots of warriors on the mountain, maybe a thousand on the mountain. Manuelito takes five hundred to attack the fort on three sides. It is in the early morning when it is still dark. The soldiers, even if they're looking out, they can't see us. There are about five hundred warriors altogether, but we split into groups. Each group has more than a hundred warriors. Our arrows just pour down like hail on that fort. Chief Manuelito is with us, and Chief Barboncito too. They set the fire on the building. The soldiers don't really come after us. They are too busy putting out the fire.

While it's still dark we take off to our hiding place. And the next morning the company of cavalry is sent to Ch'óshgai [the Chuska Mountains] in search of Manuelito's warriors. They ride through red rock country, but they can't find us anywhere. All this time we are looking at them from the top of Tséłchíí' Bee Níyołí, The-Red-Rock-Where-the-Wind-Goes-Around-It.

Chosen to Be a Leader

I am very happy my father already took me everywhere when I was young to look at all those places on the Navajo land. Now I have to fight for our land, and I already know where to hide, where to get food, where there is water.

One of the chiefs I know really well. His name is Dághaa'ii, Mustache. He has a Mexican name too—Delgadito. Manuelito and Delgadito are the chiefs of all the warriors. They have leaders under them to tell the warriors where to go. Delgadito chooses me to be a leader of the band of warriors. I think of my father's words, "Someday you'll be a brave leader." Now my father and mother are dead. I am an orphan. I remember my father's words when he was living. I remember that he took me all over the Navajo land. If it were someplace else, I would worry, but I know this land well. And I'm supposed to be brave if I'm a leader, so I just do what the chief says and take the men. I'm the head leader, and there are about seven or eight leaders that are under me to take care of all the people—the men, women, and children.

In every group there should be a runner. There always has to be somebody on hand to take a message to where the warriors are. They do it in relay on horse or on foot. Manuelito is the main leader, and he always knows where the warriors are. He sends the messenger, and within a week or so the warriors have to be ready for the attack. We are always ready. That is what we do.

There are many enemies of the Navajo: Utes, Apache, Mexican, Paiute, and Comanche. Sometimes these guys even fight

on the side of the white soldiers. The Navajo call the Comanche Naałání Dziłghą́'í. They are the meanest, most ruthless of
the enemies. They shoot anyone on sight—little kids, women
that are pregnant, and old people. One time these enemies
chased many Navajos from the Shonto area up to Navajo
Mountain. Some people went to a place called Raw-Face and
another place called Underarm. Both were canyons near
Navajo Mountain. These people stayed there for two years.

And it isn't only the other tribes we have to look out for.
Even our own people work against us. That's the way it is with
Ahidigishii. He is Navajo, the enemy of his own tribe, raiding
upon us. With him travel several men and women. They are a
tough gang. He is the leader. If they happen to come upon
someone herding sheep, they catch a sheep and butcher it and
have a feast.

There is a Navajo family on Grey Mountain that is forced to
move to Fort Defiance. They start moving east from south of
the Grand Canyon. They go through some woods, and they
come upon the camp where Ahidigishii's gang are. Ahidigishii
shoots a horse while the lady and her son are riding. The horse
falls. The lady and the son take off on foot and tell the family
what happened, and the family just stops there, and they try to
hunt for the main leader. There are two men in this family.
One man has a gun and the other has a bow and arrow. They
finally find Ahidigishii sitting on the rock. He has just finished a feast, and he is picking his teeth with a toothpick. The
men ride up to him without fear.

Hastiin Łitsoii Ts'ósí says to him, "Ahidigishii, why did you
kill our horse?" Ahidigishii won't speak a word. So Hastiin
Łitsoii Ts'ósí gets off his horse and walks up to him and
strikes him on the head with his rifle butt. Ahidigishii slumps
to the side. Hastiin Łitsoii Ts'ósí shoots him and leaves his
body there. His band disappears quickly. That is how Ahidigishii got killed. Nobody found out what clan he was. His gang
went raiding other tribes and made enemies against the Nava-

Canyon de Chelly, an oasis in the Arizona desert, is revered for the corn, beans, and fruit that can be cultivated between its rock walls.

jos. He made innocent people suffer and pay with their lives.

Sometimes the Navajo warriors who are captured give us trouble. Sometimes they tell the enemy where the hiding place is for the Navajo, how many are there, and all that. And what chief's name is there holding the warriors there. And Manuelito gets really mad to the people. He says, "Just because they capture you and even take your life, it's just you and not all your people who will suffer. When you get captured, you just tell them, 'Go ahead and kill me, and I will shed my blood on my own land, not some strange land. And my people will have the land even if *I* die.'" Manuelito talks to the people all the time. He tells them, "Love your people and love your land. We already lost our own beloved ones. But we still are on our land. There's four sacred mountains. We are supposed to be here. The Great Spirit gave the land to us. So don't tell the enemy where the warriors are. And don't give up."

There are many warriors and other chiefs besides Delgadito and Manuelito who hold onto the brave thoughts of never allowing the enemy to take the land from the people as long as any one of us is still living.

Now a messenger runner tells us the Nóóda'í (Utes) are coming to attack us. We get the message, and so we take all the kids and women and some warriors and some food and go hide in Canyon de Chelly. We are told the Utes are mean people. They got guns and arrows, and they have long hair, not tied.

In Canyon de Chelly there are families that do farming where there is enough water. They plant corn and peaches and look after the crops until they ripen. When we get to Canyon de Chelly we tell the families the enemy is coming, but some don't believe us. They keep saying, "We never do any harm to anybody." They say, "Nobody in this world will try to take away our land." We tell them to hide and take all their kids someplace to hide, but they stay. Some other families say they will go to the mountains before the winter and stay there because they don't want to see their favorite peach orchards burn.

There is another chief, Dághá Yázhí, which means Little-Beard. He has a Mexican name too—Barboncito. He and his warriors are up on top of the rim, guarding these people who are down in the canyon. Barboncito and his warriors see a wagon coming toward the canyon. They think that the wagon is going to attack the families down below, so Barboncito and his warriors attack this wagon and run the mules off to the canyon, where we use them for winter meat supply. They kill these soldiers who are coming on the wagon. They are carrying supplies for the army. Barboncito gets the horses and the supplies that they are carrying—guns too.

Canyon de Chelly is a sacred place for the Navajos. This is where the Mother Earth keeps her children hiding from the enemy. In Canyon de Chelly no enemies will kill all her children, for there are lots of hiding places. Some places the rocks are like underarms, and we call it our Mother Earth's Underarm. That is where our hiding place is. I have to find safe places for the people to hide.

Sometimes I think the Great Spirit is guiding me, telling me, "Don't go there, go this way." I think it is my father's spirit guiding me. I mean my real father—and my Father Sky.

Chief Barboncito voluntarily turned himself over to U.S. troops so he could accompany his people on the Long Walk. He gave them strength and hope during the four years of incarceration at Bosque Redondo.

The nonerosive landforms of Canyon de Chelly offered elusive hiding places to the Navajo people.

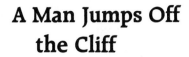

A Man Jumps Off the Cliff

One day a young warrior goes hunting for food for the people—jackrabbit or bunny rabbit or anything he could. He has bow and arrows. He goes out by himself. The leaders always tell the warriors not to go off by themselves, but this guy does it anyway. He thinks nobody would see him.

But he is spotted by the bluecoat soldiers riding horses. They chase him. The only place to go is to the cliff. He runs straight to it, and when he gets to the edge, he looks down. It is a long way down there. Then he sees a tall tree called *ch'ó deenínii* (Douglas fir). This is a young, really tall fir tree. He doesn't stop to think. He just jumps off the cliff and catches the tip of the tree, and the tree doesn't break. It just bends down like rubber. I think he has just the right weight for it. It puts him down on the ground safely, and the tree flips back up.

Just then the enemies get to the edge of the cliff. They get off their horses and look down and see the man walking away safely down the canyon. There is no way to catch him. They can't figure out how he ever got down there in the canyon.

Hiding in Canyon de Chelly

There is a certain bird that tells the Navajos the enemy is coming. This bird is called in Navajo *ts'ání dílzhi'í łichíí'* (red blue jay).[4] This bird makes a loud, pretty sound. This blue jay always flies off in the direction the enemy is coming from. We always have to have warriors on lookout for the enemy. There are three or four warriors to each hill to look for the approach of any enemy, and this bird helps us.

Everybody has to know something—maybe a ritual or a song—to be safe from the enemies or from starvation or sickness or freezing. They have to remember, keep it in their mind when the enemies are all around them.

Like when we are eating, we just make a mush with corn flour and water. We cook it in a pot and have to eat it from the pot with our finger—no dishes, no spoons. We're always in a hurry eating, worried the enemy might be close. So before we eat, we have to make a circle around the top rim of the pot with charcoal. We put the path-line around clockwise, start at the East. And we make it all around, but we don't close the circle—just leave a small space, leave it open at the East. And then we make lines on the side of the pot. The first one goes from the ground up to the circle. The next one goes from the circle down to the ground, then up, then down, and so on. We just keep on going like that all around the side of the pot,

4. Woodhouse Blue Jay.

clockwise. This is like lots of safe paths of escape. Up the mountain, down the canyon, or just anywhere to keep away from the enemy.

There is a song too. They call it a traveling song. If you know the song, wherever you go it keeps you safe. Every warrior knows a traveling song— not all the same song; they are all different. These are all carried on from their ancestors. They have to remember, keep it in their mind or sing when they are running from the enemy. This is how lots of Navajos survive.

This particular winter is very cold, and snow is deep in some places, over the ankles. We are expecting the Utes, but they don't come. We are hiding in a big cave halfway up the high cliff face, hundreds of warriors, and more than that— women and kids and husbands. We see something some miles away, moving toward us where we are hiding. We don't know what it is. It is just rolling on the old trail. At first we think it is a snowball. We have never seen such a thing. When it gets closer it is a covered wagon.

The covered wagon camps at the mouth of Canyon de Chelly. We notice it has white soldiers and Mexicans. They put up tents, some at the east end of the canyon and some at the west end. They camp there for a week. A few of the soldiers go into the canyon and destroy hogans, orchards, and livestock. They kill three Navajos trying to stop them. They capture nineteen women and children. Those families are the ones that didn't want to move. This makes us really heartaching. The soldiers leave nothing, destroy everything. They take the captured Navajos to Fort Canby.[5] Some of the warriors escape from their capture and bring the news to us.

They tell us that it is Kit Carson that orders complete destruction of Navajo properties within the canyon. Once Kit Carson was our good friend. We called him Rope-Thrower. He

5. Fort Defiance was called Fort Canby during the years 1863 and 1864.

could do tricks with the rope; that is why we called him that. We never think of him as a soldier, as fighting against us or taking us prisoners. We Navajos will never have the heart to forgive Kit Carson—he has done the damage already.

The messengers tell us to go ahead and fight. The next day we start our ambush on both ends of the canyons. The soldiers use guns. We use bows and arrows. Our warriors chase part of them back. The next day everything is quiet, but we still have to keep our warriors there.

There are some bands of warriors all over the Navajo land. We send messages to them that the enemies are over here. Warriors come to help. They scout the canyon from the rim. The enemy keeps trying very hard to get in the canyon, and they get on their horses and fire at our cave. Our Navajo warriors shoot back with bows and arrows. We don't have lots of guns, maybe only five guns to each group of a hundred warriors. There are lots of men and women and children that get killed. People are lying everywhere. One of the leaders under me gets so mad, and he takes some warriors down from the cave, and they fight with the soldiers on the ground. There are lots of Navajo killed here. Many are wounded.

While all this fighting is down there, some of the people up in the cave want to jump off so they don't get shot or captured. Mostly it is the kids and women that are scared that do this. The warriors have to push the people back from jumping off the cliff. Still, some families just jump down, because they don't want to be shot by the enemy. They commit suicide. They think there is no way to be safe. It is very hard for us warriors to save the people. The people are pushing themselves to the edge, and pushing us too. Even though we are strong, it is hard to hold them back. Some warriors get shot from the ground when they are pushing the people back.

I am crying. I feel sorry for our people that are killing themselves. We warriors are supposed to be brave, and we are not supposed to cry. But it is very scary to see the families jump

*Kit Carson, once a friend of the Navajo, later commanded U.S. troops
to round up and incarcerate them.*

off the cliff. We try to talk to them, to tell them to stay back
from the cliff edge. We tell them not to do that because someday it will be peace. Our Great Spirit will save us, some way
or other. I save some of the lives by talking to them like that.
I have to talk to them from my heart, not just my lips.

I think of my parents. Where would they be if they were
alive? I think when you are an orphan, that makes you strong.
There are many warriors like me. We all try to save the people.
I always think they are all my parents. I love them all. I don't
want to see them get killed. Bad enough we see them get shot.
Worse to see them killing themselves by jumping off the cliff.

There is a dreadful fighting right in front of our eyes. Pretty
soon the leader of the white soldiers commands to cease fire.
He is frightened. He breaks down and weeps, saying, "What a
terrible thing we have done to these people."

The soldiers go back to the camp, and after a little while
they come back with a white flag. Two Navajos who were captured are used for interpreters. The soldiers say, "We will not

fight no more." They say, "Go to the camp and talk with the leader, and he will give you peace."

When the Navajo warriors get to the camp to talk with the leader, the white soldier points a gun at them and they go in the tent. The white leader starts crying again. He says, "I am very sorry what tragic event I have caused." They make an agreement. There will be no more fighting. The white leader tells them go to Fort Defiance to get the free food.

The white soldier doesn't know there is a tragic journey in the future for the Navajos. He thinks he is giving them good advice to pay back their loss—the people who got killed—to get free food.

The Navajo warriors tell this white leader they are suffering and dying from hunger. After they talk with the leader, the soldiers give them some food for the people that survived. And they give them a white flag and tell them, "Just move to Fort Defiance. That way the enemy won't bother you anymore. The white flag means peace, or you need help." This is what the leader says to them.

The Navajo warriors go back and tell their people, "Don't be afraid. There is no enemy, and you should move to Fort Defiance." Some of the families do move to Fort Defiance, and they get free food. But the food isn't the kind they think it should be. They don't like the food. They don't know how to cook it. The coffee is just beans. They just boil it the way it is until somebody tells them they should grind the coffee beans, then boil them. So that makes coffee. And the salty bacon. They don't know how to cook it too. Some of them boil the salty bacon, and they get stomachaches. They have a hard time with the food to get used to it. And there is cornmeal too. It isn't ground good too. They have to eat it—nothing else to eat.

Everybody still in the canyon gets a message from the white leader from Fort Defiance: "There will be no more killing." Lots of the families and warriors don't believe it, and they stay in the canyon. There's lots of places they hide. And Manuelito just sends even more warriors down into the canyon.

But some more of the families do go over to Fort Defiance to see what is going on and to get free food. It is the same at Shash Bitoo, Fort Wingate.[6] People go for food and aren't let to go home.

The soldiers tell them they are being punished for raiding around to all the tribes. All the tribes have told the soldiers, "The Navajos are taking sheep and horse and cattle, taking them away to their land."

The Navajos tell the soldiers that it is just a handful of Navajos starting the raids, not all the Navajos. But all the Navajos are being punished—they are punished for what they didn't do. Here those few Navajos are making enemies all over and making innocent people suffer and pay with their lives. The Navajos say to the soldiers they should punish just the troublemakers.

Manuelito and Barboncito get a message from Fort Wingate. It says there's already lots of people over there at Fort Wingate. Barboncito goes with his warriors to see how many are there. When they get close to Fort Wingate, the soldiers see them and put them in jail at Fort Wingate.

When Manuelito gets the news that Barboncito is in jail, he says, "I will be next to be hunted down." He had heard that General Carleton had given orders to hunt him and his warriors. Carleton had said he wanted Manuelito and his warriors

6. Two forts bore the name Fort Wingate during the Bosque Redondo period. One, labeled Fort Wingate I on Map 2, was established in 1862. The other (Fort Wingate II) was named Fort Lyon when it was established in 1861, but it was renamed when the garrison of the original Fort Wingate was transferred there in 1868. Thus, when the text refers to Fort Wingate prior to the Bosque Redondo period, the reference is to Fort Wingate I. When Gus Bighorse refers to Fort Wingate later, however, it is unclear which fort is meant.

dead or alive. But Manuelito tells his warriors to keep hiding. He says, "They already took part of our people and put them in prison. What more do they want? We love this land, and we have to keep ourselves brave to keep the land and help each other to stay free." The next Manuelito hears, Barboncito and his bands have escaped from prison. They were never captured again.

The Long Walk
to Hwéeldi

The white message-carriers even take the message clear to Grey Mountain, where the people are picking piñons. These families hide their piñons. What they have picked, they hide it and go to get some free food at Fort Defiance. Here these families think they will come back and pick up their piñons. When they get there, there are lots of people over there at Fort Defiance and very little food.

Over there at Fort Defiance they are told they have to go to Hwéeldi [Fort Sumner].[7] These families just ask the white leader to let them go and pick up the piñons that they left on the mountain, and he won't let them go. He just says, "Nobody comes out from this fort. Nobody."

The father of the family thinks it was a terrible idea to have come. He never dreamed of something like this happening. I don't know how long they stayed there before the soldiers herded them together and the Long Walk begins. The father of the family feels really bad. He should have kept his family to pick piñons instead of coming all the way to Fort Defiance to get free food.

The snow is still on the ground and the trees are just getting green when the Navajo are told they will soon have to move to Fort Sumner. Food and care and protection are promised by the white leader. The soldiers tell the Navajo to follow orders,

7. The Navajos were sent to Bosque Redondo, an area of approximately twenty square miles along the Pecos River (New Mexico). Fort Sumner was located within this area. The term Hwéeldi, as used by the Navajo, designates the entire area without differentiating between Fort Sumner and Bosque Redondo.

then everything will go well. They don't know how many days
it will take them to walk.

Manuelito, Barboncito, and all the warriors talk for several
days. Manuelito gives an order to Barboncito to take some
warriors and go along with his people so he can give them en-
couragement. Also, Barboncito should send messages back to
Manuelito to tell him what is going on. Barboncito says he
will go with his people because the enemy is taking his people
to a place nobody knows about.

Manuelito stays with the people that are not yet captured—
those still in hiding. Manuelito promises Barboncito's warriors
that he will never give up his land or give up on his people.
He says he would rather stay and die in his own land that he
loves. Manuelito says, "I have nothing to lose but my life, and
they can come and take that any time that they want to." He
says, "I will not move from where I was born in the Chuska
Mountains, where the Great Spirit put me." So Barboncito and
some of his warriors surrender with some women and children
and go to Fort Defiance with lots of Navajos.

The Long Walk is a tragic journey over frozen snow and
rough rocks. There are a few wagons to haul some food and
some things that belong to the white soldiers. The trip is on
foot. People are shot down on the spot if they say they are
tired or sick or if they stop to help someone. If a woman is in
labor with a baby, she is killed. There is absolutely no mercy.
Many get sick and get diarrhea because of the food. They are
heartbroken because their families die on the way. Right outside Fort Defiance when the trip just starts, they sleep there
and leave lots of bodies there. That's the way it is for the rest
of the trip. There are bodies here and there and everywhere
along the trail. About four thousand Navajos make the walk
from Fort Defiance to Fort Sumner.

Barboncito is glad he is with the people, and some warriors
that are with him are really a great help to the people. Barboncito doesn't get tired, and he just helps everyone on their feet

so they don't get shot. Barboncito gets on friendly terms with the captain. He gets the captain to agree to let the kids take turns riding on the wagon when they get tired, and the adults too. Some old men and old ladies, they have a hard time. Barboncito doesn't know how long it is going to take. He just has to keep the people going. He just has to keep giving them courage to keep on their feet. Even then they get homesick. They think they have lost their land and their families. Barboncito is glad when they get there so the people can rest, even if it is a terrible place to be. He is glad not to lose everybody. Barboncito says, "Manuelito is a really kind man and really cares for his people. Otherwise he wouldn't have sent us with the people." When the Navajos arrive at Hwéeldi, no other people live there. They have to dig holes in the ground for their shelter.

During this whole time Barboncito somehow is able to send messages back to Manuelito about the people and what is going on. I don't know how they do it. Somehow there is always someone who can get through.

The messengers get word to Manuelito. There are thirty wagons and four thousand Navajo and lots of cavalry horses. But only the cavalry can ride. There are lots of sheep and goats. The end of April, another group of people, about the same amount, make another Long Walk from Fort Wingate to Fort Sumner. The messengers tell Manuelito that there are now lots of people at Hwéeldi, maybe more than eight thousand in captivity.

A year after they get there, more soldiers come into Fort Sumner. So the soldiers make the Navajo people help make houses for the soldiers. They made them out of boards. The Navajo are like slaves to the soldiers. Build houses, chop wood—whatever chores they want them to do, the people just have to do it. The soldiers just live in those houses. But the Navajos have to live outside in the cold, in the holes in the ground.

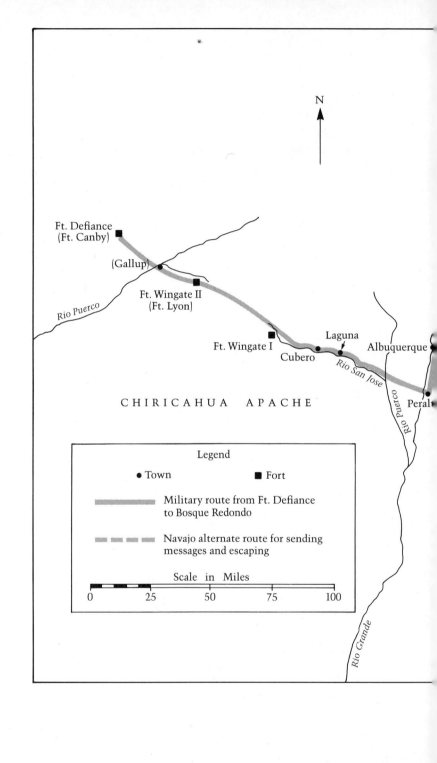

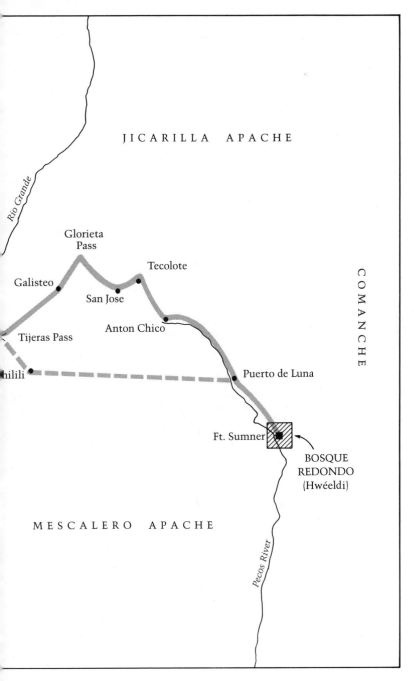

Map 2. The Route of the Long Walk

Conditions for the Navajo at Bosque Redondo were deplorable. Their food and living quarters were meager.

At Bosque Redondo, under the surveillance of armed troops, the Navajos were forced to build adobe structures for soldiers' use. These large buildings with windows, doors, and fireplaces are in clear contrast to the "holes in the ground" in which the Navajos had to live.

Hiding Behind
the Mountain

But there are Navajos that don't get captured. They are hiding in Grand Canyon, and on top of Black Mesa near Kayenta, and down to Colorado River in their own homeland. And all this time, war is going on. All the warriors are in hiding with Manuelito, and some of them are guarding him not to get killed.

One day Manuelito comes to talk to me. He tells me to take my warriors and lots of families and move over there to Colorado River behind Navajo Mountain. He says, "You will be the leader to these families and warriors. The families have to hide down there and plant food." We stay there four years, all the time Hwéeldi is going on. All that time we have to guard the families from the rim of the river. The families plant corn down there, and watermelon, even peaches. That's how they support the warriors.

Here are some warriors that stay up in the mountains with me; there are many more:

Hastiin Deenásts'aa'	Ram-Sheep
Hastiin Bilátsoohii	Big-Thumb
Hastiin Bizhí Dizhah	Big-Voice
Hastiin Ayóo Ndiilii	Big-Man
Hastiin Hadah Adeetiin	Road-Goes-Down
Hastiin Bilį́į́' Łání	Many-Horses
Hastiin Tádídínii	Corn-Pollen
Hastiin Hadilch'áłí Sání	Old-Talker
Hastiin Bilį́į́' Łizhiní	Black-Horse
Hastiin Bilį́į́' Łigaii	White-Horse

Hastiin Bidzaanézii	Mule
Hastiin Lók'aa'ch'égaii	Lukachukai
Hastiin Tł'aashchí'í	Red-Bottom-People Clan
Hastiin Ntł'aaí	Left-Handed
Hastiin Tł'ízí Łání	Many-Goats
Hastiin Atsą́ą́' Béheestł'ónii	Ribs-Tied-To
Hastiin Tódích'íi'nii Sání	Old-Bitter-Water
Hastiin Tł'ahnii Bidághaa' Łichíi'ii	Left-Handed-Red-Whiskers
Hastiin Yistł'inii	Spotted-Man
Hastiin Bitł'ízí Łigaii	White-Goats
Hastiin Tł'aaí Nééz	Tall-Lefthanded
Hastiin Béégashii Łání	Much-Cattle
Hastiin Ndaaz	Heavy
Hastiin Biłóodii	Sore
Hastiin Nééz	Tall-Man
Hastiin Béésh Łigaii	Silversmith
Hastiin Béésh Łigaii Yitsidí	White-Silversmith
Hastiin Bigodí	Wounded-Knee
Hastiin Chishí Nééz	[Navajo clan]
Hastiin Bidághaa' Łitso	Light-Beard

From time to time new people come in our camp. They bring their family and their herds and tell us the story of how they get over here and how they get away from the enemy. Here is Hastiin Bigodí's story:

He is living on the west side of Black Mountain. He is a medicine man, and people call him Hataałii. He is living peacefully on the other side of the mountain. He is head of about seven families, and they have livestock and horses and mules and donkeys. They live in one place for about five years, and they herd their livestock on the mountain in the summer, and they bring them down in the fall. He doesn't know some Navajos are having trouble with all these different tribes of Indians, or there is killing going on.

One day, somebody brings him bad news. That there are soldiers who are going to kill all the Navajos. He tells his family to move toward Navajo Mountain, all together. While they are moving in a bunch, the dust rises from the herds of sheep and horses, and they are seen by the soldiers. Some families don't move fast enough. They get trapped by the soldiers, who catch them and force them to Fort Defiance. Men get killed while protecting their herds and their families. Hataałii is way ahead with three families, and they get away. They go to a canyon just before Navajo Mountain. It is a long way from Black Mountain to Navajo Mountain. They stay there for nearly a year, and they hear that lots of Navajo are going to hide behind Navajo Mountain. But some have already gone to Fort Defiance.

One day, Hataałii goes out of the canyon to see what's going on. He runs about four or five miles. He doesn't realize that he has run that far. He runs from hill to hill. Then he sees a herd of Navajo horses running. Soldiers are riding behind the horses. He hides behind a bush.

He spends a night there, and next day he sees something moving across the wash from where he is walking. He runs to hide and throws himself in another bush. That's where he gets shot. The soldiers think he is killed—don't come to see, just leave.

He stays there for two days. He is shot up above the knee, but the bullet doesn't hit the bone. He crawls around there to find a medicine plant to put on it. He is okay then, and he can find water and some berries to eat. And he finally finds strong sticks to walk with. So he starts back toward his camp down in the canyon.

He has been gone for four days, and there are four men of his family searching for him. When he gets back near the canyon, he knows somebody is looking for him. The men have been searching for a day, but they can't find him. This day they try

again. They don't dare yell or make a fire. They think the enemies are near. These men have bows and arrows, and they
walk close together. They think he isn't close by. While they
walk they listen to every sound. One man hears somebody
calling out. They stop and look around. Hataałii is sitting on a
rock on top of a little hill. He has just gone up there to see
around. They go up to him. His body is okay, but just his knee
is wounded. Then one man says to him, "Your name will be
Hastiin Bigodí (Wounded-Knee)." He gets his name like that.

One man from the camp has brought an extra horse for
Wounded-Knee, and he gets on and they all take off. When
they get back, all the families are really happy to see him.
They all talk about how lucky he is—the bullet missed his
bone, just went through his flesh.

The next day a messenger comes to the camp. Manuelito
wants them to move behind Navajo Mountain. They leave
right away. They move their herd all night till they get to the
foot of the mountain. They rest for a day, and the next day get
down into the canyon with us. Lots of people are already here.

We tell him the Navajos left for Hwéeldi three days ago, and
the soldiers are looking all over for the Navajos that are hiding.
Wounded-Knee says, "We are here in a safe place now." He
holds a prayer for all the people—those that are here, and
those that are still hiding in the canyon, and those that are
marching to Hwéeldi. He prays they will be safely returned to
their land.

He is a young man about thirty-four years old. He knows
lots of stories. He knows how to make saddles and bridles and
how to braid ropes from hides. He likes to tease around, and
everybody calls him Our Son-in-Law.

His families bring lots of livestock into the canyon. They
tell us, "We found lots of sheep and goats down in that canyon.
Nobody was around. Maybe the people who went to Hwéeldi
lost their herds. Maybe the herds got frightened and ran into

the canyon. So we just put the sheep and goats with our herd. I think they were put there for us to bring them here to help us survive. We should all think about how we will survive. I don't know how long we will be here, and we men down here have to get to work and feed our warriors good so they will be strong and healthy. They are not afraid to fight. They can face their enemies face-to-face to fight them. And we have our work to do too." And he lets the boys clear the bushes where they will plant. Just a few days later the ground is all ready to plant on.

The people at the camp always listen to him. He is a great man, and he can say a kind word to the people that lose their relatives and those that their men get killed by the soldiers. He says, "We lost lots of our relatives. Some of them are killed and some are forced to go to Fort Defiance. But we are all here, and we all are in one family. We love each other and will help each other."

We warriors know him really well. He comes and talks to us too. He is always saying, "Thank you very much for your guarding us." Sometimes he brings lots of food for us to eat. He is young but wise.

All these people behind Navajo Mountain are wondering when these people will return to their homeland from Hwéeldi. The medicine man named Many-Whiskers and another called Old-Arrow go to the top of Navajo Mountain to pray to the Holy People. They pray that these captured Navajos will come back to their homeland safely, soon be free. At this time there are lots of medicine men. They pray every time before they eat—the whole family, all the time praying for the safe return. When they cook mush or any kind of corn food to eat, they use the stick, *ádístsiin*, that they stir it with. When they are finished, they take that stick out, with the mush on it, and they pray with it, too, for the safe return. And they can pray to the fire too. The charcoal that they use to cook with, they pray with it for their people to come home safely. They use corn pollen. And some of them use the corn that's ground. They do this every day and every night, before the sunset and after the sunset—white corn before the sunset, and yellow corn after the sunset. And they pray for the warriors that are protecting them and for the white people who are holding all those people captive, pray to soften the white soldiers' hearts to let these people go free.

Tséghą́ą́'

The Ute are hired by the
government in Washing-
ton and paid by it to help
scout with the soldiers to
take Navajos as captives.
They take soldiers to Canyon de
Chelly to look for the Navajos.
When we are at Navajo
Mountain, a message
comes to us. A runner tells
us about what is happening
over there at Tséghą́ą́'.
Tséghą́ą́' means On-
Top-of-the-Rock. It is a big rock-cliff, flat on top and separate
from the sides of the canyon. There are water holes, *tsé'ézis*,
on top, like bowls. There's lots of them like this all over, and
the rain and snow can melt in there to make lots of water.

This place on top of the rock was found by some warriors.
There were about one hundred men who started working on it,
figuring how to get up there themselves, and how to get the
families up there. They worked on it for many days. They
made two ladders—long ones. And they made holes in the
rock so they can put their feet in there to climb the rock. And
they even take some firewood and some food up there.

The runner says that there are lots of people up there, and
the enemies can't reach them. There are about two hundred
warriors up there. They have some rifles, plenty of bows and
arrows. They use a ladder to get up there, but the ladder can be

pulled to the top of the rock, so no enemy could get to them.

The messenger runner says to us, "You, too, are in a safe place. No enemy will come this way. I myself had a hard time finding you. Over at Tséghą́ą́' the people are safe too. Don't worry about them. And they got food too. They are with lots of warriors to protect them."

Delgadito is the leader of the people who moved on top of Tséghą́ą́'. They can't take their livestock with them, so they leave them in the canyon where no enemy can find them. Delgadito tells his people to be strong and help each other. "We have to leave some men to take care of the sheep." He says, "We don't know how long we will be up there. We have to butcher some sheep to take the meat with us. And when we are out of meat, somebody will have to come down and get some more meat." That is what they do. And there are lots of warriors, and they have to feed them good, so they can protect the people. Navajo women, men, and children—they always look up to Delgadito. They think of him as a great leader, even though he is a small man.

One day much later, Hastiin Jaatł'óół Nineezí, Mr. Long-Earring, rides a horse to our warriors' camp behind Navajo Mountain. He says he has been staying at Tséghą́ą́' for quite a while. He tells us he was witness. Some Navajos got killed down on the ground, close to Tséghą́ą́'. He tells us that after all the people got up on top, it was quiet for a number of days. With the children, women, men, and warriors, it was three hundred people on top of Tséghą́ą́'. All the warriors had to help each other to get some firewood on top of the rock. They couldn't even make smoke for fear the soldiers would see it.

It was Kit Carson that gave orders to his soldiers to come to Tséghą́ą́', but they had no way of attacking the people on top. They couldn't get up there, and it was too far to shoot. The soldiers just stayed in the canyon for two or three days and left. Nobody bothered the livestock, either.

The Navajo lived close to the earth—its plants and animals. Their bows, arrows, deerskin moccasins, turquoise ornaments, and plant-dyed blankets were gifts from the land.

Kit Carson kept searching out the Navajos—to kill them if
he saw them. But he and his soldiers didn't go as far as Navajo
Mountain. Kit Carson went through Dinnebito to Kayenta
area. The soldiers searched all over for the Navajos. Through
Steamboat Canyon and Ganado area and Wide Ruin and back
to Fort Defiance. They quit scouting around and reported back
to their headquarters. There was not a sign of Navajos. Searching was useless.

Living at Hwéeldi

It's really dangerous to send messages from Hwéeldi to Manuelito. On the Navajo land the soldiers are trying to hunt down Manuelito to kill him and his warriors. Every once in a while some fast runners escape from the camp and bring messages to Manuelito. Then he goes around to where the warriors are and tells them the news. Some bands he tells to stay there, and some bands he tells to go someplace else. He always knows where they are and brings them news about what is happening at Hwéeldi.

At Hwéeldi the Navajos have to walk four or five miles to find wood. That is the nearest. Some of them have to walk fifteen miles to find firewood. They have to dig out mesquite roots. These are hard to find. Two men start early in the morning, come back after midnight to bring back a little bundle of firewood. The people are suffering their worst hardships in winter when it gets really cold.

The food is grass seeds, yucca fruit, piñon nuts, wild berries, cedar tree berries. The water is not good too. Large numbers of Navajo are starving to death. In the second year and third year, the people are forced to plant corn and watermelon. It doesn't grow. They are told to plant the corn in white man's way. Still doesn't grow. The soil isn't good, and the grasshoppers eat the seeds.

Some Navajos say that even if the corn grows it will be for the armies, not them. So they think maybe that is why the corn doesn't grow. They just have to stay with the salted bacon and cornmeal to keep themselves alive.

Barboncito and his warriors go around to talk to the people. They tell them they should help each other like they are all part of the same family. Everybody help each other so they don't lose more lives. "Keep on praying," he tells them. "The Great Spirit is listening, so pray." Without Barboncito and his warriors, the people would never make it.

Here is what the messengers tell about Hwéeldi, and more:

The Comanche tribe is the meanest tribe to the Navajo. They come to the Navajo camp at Hwéeldi. They tell the Navajo this land belongs to them. The wood belongs to them. The water belongs to them. The hunting grounds belong to them. The Navajo believe them, and they think they live in Comanche land. The Comanches come to the camp every day and steal the Navajo livestock. The Navajo live in fear for four years because their enemies are all around them and armed, and the Navajos are not armed. The people can't complain to the soldiers. The soldiers just let the Comanches come in and steal everything from the Navajo.

The Navajo brought a great number of stock with them on the Long Walk and lost them. Nearly all of them died. That left the Navajo so poor. Some Navajos were well off. Now they got nothing. They don't have no blankets. All they have to sleep with is gunnysacks.

Mostly half of the Navajos die over there at Hwéeldi. Every day they look around and see everybody so weak and sick. There's so many people packed together, no clean place to go to the bathroom, not much clothes. Everybody so cold, hungry, and thin. They don't even look like themselves. Every day they think maybe this will be the last day that they see each other. Maybe there won't be another day.

The chiefs worry all the time. If the people stay there a little longer, they will starve. Barboncito is very sad about his people and how they are suffering, but he tells them, "We are going back to our own land. Don't give up. Make yourself strong."

The Chiefs
Sign the Treaty

One day Barboncito sends a message from Hwéeldi to Manuelito and Delgadito to come to Fort Sumner and sign a treaty. The treaty is to release the people. It is an agreement between the parties that forever they will not have war again. So Manuelito holds a meeting with his warriors to talk about the message. He tells them, "This is the fourth treaty they want me to sign. I already signed three others. And every time it's broken by the white soldiers." So they talk about it all day and all night, and he is saying, "Do you think it's okay if I go over there? Do you think those soldiers just want me to get out of my hiding place? To kill me? Do you think the treaty won't be broken again?" This is the way he talks.

And some of these warriors are medicine men, and when they talk about their ceremonies and sing to an evil spirit, they say something four times. Always in ceremony, four is a sacred number. Everything is done four times. Once for the East, once for the South, once for the West, once for the North. So they talk about it like that. Maybe this treaty will be Truth and won't be broken. It's the fourth one.

In these days when something big is to be done, the warriors have to be talking all night to get agreement on one subject. That is what they do at this meeting. And some warriors dream about the treaty, and they dream that it will never break again. In these days they follow the dream. If it's bad, somebody has to pray for you so what's in the dream will never happen. This time the dream is good, and they agree Manuelito should go.

All the ladies hold onto him, because the ladies and men think they will lose him if the soldiers kill him. But Manuelito says, "I will go. Let the soldiers see my face again. Maybe this treaty will never break."

So Manuelito chooses some warriors to go with him, and he tells me to stay with the families and warriors at Navajo Mountain—the ones that never were found by the cavalry. He tells me, "Stay with your people and stand guard till we come back and tell you what happened."

Manuelito takes some warriors to Fort Sumner. I don't know how many days they ride. They take extra horses. Manuelito takes his wife, Juanita. She is a very tough lady. She is brave and uses guns and bows and arrows. She is always by Manuelito, her husband.

When they get to Fort Sumner, Manuelito is really upset with the soldiers. Now Manuelito knows how far his people walked. He thinks the ones that survived must be very strong and tough. He can't really recognize his relatives and his people that he knew before. They're so thin and have been suffering so much all this time.

The people plead to Manuelito to hurry and sign the treaty. Everybody is crying—they want to go home. Barboncito and his warriors try to keep the people calm.

Manuelito, Delgadito, Barboncito, and the warriors all talk with the captain and the leader of the army. They want to hear what the leaders are saying. They want to know what they are signing. They want to be sure the treaty won't be broken.

And the Navajos don't speak English. They just have a Mexican interpreter. The Washington bosses tell them that the treaty means peace. There will be no more fighting. They just have to go back to their homeland and live in peace, and put their kids in school for education. And there's a boundary line that they have to obey. They can't go outside the boundary line except to trade with other Indians, Mexicans, or white men.

Manuelito asks the Washington bosses, "Where shall the

kids go to school?" They tell him, "The schools will be at Chinle and Fort Wingate." They just name two places. The chief says that it shouldn't be far away from the Navajo land, otherwise the Navajo won't put their kids in school. The people will think that the soldiers are taking their kids away from them like the soldiers did to them, taking them to Hwéeldi. So Manuelito says to them, "When we put the kids in school, are you going to mistreat them like you did us?" And the Washington bosses say, "No, they just have to go to school to learn English. They will get food and clothes and a place to sleep. These things will be coming from the government, and the kids won't be mistreated."

They have a meeting all day. Barboncito tells the bosses from Washington how much the Navajo have suffered, how much they have lost, that they tried to plant the corn, but it didn't grow good. He tells them, "Here we've done all the things you told us to do, and we had lots of suffering. We want to go home, all of us." He is talking for the people, and he is wanting the white bosses from Washington to know everything that happened.

Manuelito is so mad at the suffering, but he has to keep himself calm. He wants the people to go home.

There are ten Navajo chiefs and leaders. They all agree and sign the treaty. They just make an x, and the bluecoat captains witness the signing, and each just writes the Navajo leader's name beside their x. And the chiefs give messages to runners to be taken to all parts of the Indian country to notify them of the treaty.

Coming Back to the Homeland

Our people are released from a land they never will call theirs. They will never forget what happened to half of their people in front of their very eyes. They had witnessed every person that suffered the death of starvation and sickness and cold and heartbreak and mistreatment from their enemies.

The survivors are now free to return to their beloved homeland. The people are so excited, they can't wait to get started, to see their relatives that they left behind. Even if it is a long way back, they are praying that they can make it and look over their land.

The government just gives them sheep and goats to start to make a flock again, but no food. Maybe they think the Navajo won't make it back home. Here they are free but have to suffer more, because they don't have any food.

And the chiefs go with them to lead them back. The soldiers tell the chiefs they should lead their people the same way they came to Fort Sumner. The chiefs that are there tell the people, "Don't hurry, just take your time. You will be there. Don't get yourself tired out." They just want all the people to reach their own land without any trouble.

Lots of people don't make it. It takes fifteen days, some of them twenty days. They have to rest their horses and sheep. At night they stay where there is grass for the horses and sheep, and water too.

One old lady sees Mount Taylor from the distance—the sacred mountain of the South—just half of the mountain sticking out. She starts crying, "Mountain! We are home!" and she faints. Then she gets really sick, and she dies two days later—dies from being so happy.

The chiefs are sorry. They are saying, "We don't want to lose anybody, because the relatives are waiting to see us." They bury the lady and go on again. They have to be very careful with those old men and women.

It is just like when they were going to Fort Sumner. A lot of people can't make it. They have to go all the way to Fort Defiance. Some of them are naked. They only have a *tł'eestsooz*, a breechcloth—whatever could be found to wear on the front. And they are barefooted.

But some of the old people can't walk any farther. They stay behind and begin living near Albuquerque. Old men, medicine men, conduct ceremonies asking the Holy People to bless them and the sheep and goats and horses and water and land and farmland and the grazing land.

When the people are coming back from Hwéeldi, some warriors are still in the mountains. The messengers bring them the good news—the treaty is signed and the people are coming back. Some of the warriors don't believe it and won't come down from the mountains.

Manuelito gathers all his warriors and some families that are there. We all get together and talk with the chiefs and warriors from Hwéeldi about what happened over there. We stay in that camp for six days. Day and night we are talking about the tragic things that happened. Four years in a strange land.

And there's one captain the people didn't like. His name is
Carl.[8] That's what they called him at that time. He treated
them like a dog and always pushed them around. Our interpreter told us that Carl got in an argument with another captain. The captain told him to let the people go home, but Carl
said no. He won't let them. He wants to keep the people there.
He wants the people to starve there. He doesn't want them to
go back home. That's why they don't like him.

"Sometimes we couldn't stand him. We wished to hit him
or something. To make him suffer. But we didn't have enough
strength or something to do it." That's what the chief said.
"Carl always ate lots of food, and he had a big stomach. He
sure could stand against us to talk to us like that. He wasn't
even hungry, and we were starving, so he didn't even feel it.

"If somebody died in the hogan, we didn't want to sleep in
there. But that Carl always pushed the people in the place
where the person died. He said there was nothing wrong
with it."

We Navajos always think that the person that died, his
ch'įįdii, evil spirit, is still in there. Or whatever he died of, you
might catch it, just like a disease. Don't go in there. You might
catch it. That's why they don't like it. Till a few days later,
they can. But not just right away. "So," the chiefs said, "we
never slept in there even if it was cold outside. We just slept
out there."

And we talk about how the treaty was signed. They are saying this is the fourth time they sign the treaty. Maybe this is a
true one. Maybe it will not be broken again.

Manuelito tells us the treaty means we have to put our kids
in school. Some of the people don't like it. They want to keep
their kids home, to know a Navajo way more than school. And
about the school at Chinle and Fort Wingate, some don't like
that too. It's too far from home. Some people will have to go

8. Brigadier General James H. Carleton.

all the way across the Navajo land to take their kids to school. That's why they don't like it.

But Barboncito tells them, "When we were over there at Fort Sumner, none of us talk English. It was too hard for us. We had to get an interpreter. It was a Mexican guy that was talking for us. And it was good that the Mexican guy was with us. But sometimes we didn't believe what the soldiers really said to us. It was too hard for us to understand what was going on. We were just blank. So just put your kids in school, and someday we'll have lots of interpreters. We never went to school, and now we're too old. But when you put your kids in school, someday there will be lots of English talkers."

And we talk about how happy we are that the people came back. Now we believe the message. Now we think the treaty is Truth, and we are happy about it.

So Chief Manuelito tells us to lay our weapons down and go make a living. But he says, "Just in case, have your weapons ready all the time."

We go to all directions. We take our tragic story with us, but we can't talk about it. It is so terrible. Only if somebody would ask us a question, then we talk about it.

How I Got This Bullet

One day I get up early in the morning. I decide to look for my horses. This is after the treaty is signed. I think I go out in the open space too early.

I run about two miles from where I live. I find my horses. There are eight of them. I catch one. I have a little yucca-plant braid string. I tie the yucca string to one side of the horse's muzzle. Just then I hear a noise. The horses hear the noise too, and start to run. I jump on the horse's back. I hear the sound of horses' hooves a little way behind a hill. Whoever it is hasn't seen me, so I don't sit up straight, I just lay alongside of the horse, with one leg thrown over the horse's back. I'm holding tightly onto the mane, and the horses are running close together and very fast. I hear men and horses coming after me, and then I hear a shot. It scares the horses, and they run so fast I can't even see the ground.

My hands are tired from holding on. I jump down and run for safety. I run in a little wash. I think to myself, I'll get killed here. The Mexicans will kill me, instead of the blue-clothes soldiers. I stand there and just say a little prayer, trying to catch my breath. I turn around. There are three men.

They stop a little ways from me, but they don't get off their horses. They just stay on and smile and say, "Amigo." Amigo means friend. Then they point their finger to the south and say "Mexico," showing me they are going back home. I understand just a little bit of Spanish and nod my head. They turn around and take off.

Here I thought I was going to get killed, but I didn't. They just leave me alone. I'm happy I didn't get shot. I sit down. That is when I feel something on my rib. I feel around. I got a bullet between my skin and my rib.

I hadn't even felt it, and they don't even know they shot me. I think they just wanted to scare the horses. Maybe it was the bullet that made me tired holding onto the horse. Here I thought I had to jump down and let them shoot me. I thought, I will be killed in my own land.

I just keep thinking about it. Maybe the horse saved my life. It was running so fast the bullet didn't really reach me very good. And then I think some more. Here there's been all this fighting all around here. All the blue-clothes soldiers shooting at us, and all this time I never get in front of the bullet. But this time it's different. It's the Mexicans that give me a bullet, and they are just trying to scare the horses or turn them around. And I nearly get killed by the friendly Mexicans.

It's not the end of my life. I thank my Mother Earth and my Father Sky for saving me. I thank whoever is guiding me as long as I live. And from then on I live with a Mexican bullet on my rib.

Unrest

Two years after the Navajos came back from Hwéeldi, everybody moves away from the mountain to make a living. They move where they can find water and a place to plant corn or watermelon or pumpkins.

Everybody, everywhere, making a living, and some still searching for their relatives that went to Hwéeldi, seeing if they came back.

There are people all over the Navajo reservation. Some go east. Some stay close together where they are. Some live in fear. Some are saying, "There are no enemies," and some are saying, "Somehow, someway, some tribe will start a war again. Maybe it is not just the white soldiers, but someone." Some of the people are still keeping bows and arrows always ready.

I am with some relatives that I know real well behind Navajo Mountain. We all move to this place called Tsé Ani'įįhí, Thief Rock, near Shonto, Arizona. And we find a place with real wet soil. We clear all the bushes, using an ax to chop them out. There aren't many bushes. When we are through, it is a big place. It is spring, and we plant corn and watermelon. We use seeds that we have saved from before, when we were behind Navajo Mountain.

And we make our hogans close by. There are about three families that live near each other but separate. Our chief tells us we should stay together so we can help each other, so this is what we do. We all work in the big field—hoe it and keep it clear of the wild weeds. We do this all spring and summer.

In the middle of the summer, when the corn is ripe, somebody comes and tells us the bad news. He says, "Somebody killed a white man. Two of them. They were riding horses. These two Navajo men were chasing them way in the other valley. The two white men didn't stay together, just split up. The two Navajo men caught up with one of the white men. One of the Navajo men killed the white man and took his horse and saddle and everything. And the other white man thought he got away from the killers. But the other Navajo man didn't get anything from the guy that got killed, so he took off after the other white man. He wanted to kill him and get a horse and everything like the other Navajo did. So he hunted the white man, followed him for a long time. Close to Kayenta, he caught him and killed him.

"A Mexican man and two Navajos were riding around. They saw this second white man get killed. From a distance, they saw the killer bury his body, take his saddle and his horse and his gun. The two Navajos that were watching knew him, and when the killer left, they went over there. There was nothing there that belonged to the dead man.

"So the two Navajos and the Mexican just talked things over with each other. They asked each other if they should tell the troops that are still at Fort Wingate about the killing. The troops had said there should be no more killing, but these men said to each other, 'If we tell on this man, he will be after us all our life. But if we don't tell the troops, they will be after everybody again. Like they did before. There will be a war again.' Everything was going in their mind like that. Everybody was living in fear of another war. Then they said, 'But the killer didn't see us. He doesn't know anybody was looking at him. He doesn't know we saw him bury the body. Maybe he won't know that we are the ones that told the troops on him.

"And the Mexican man said, 'It is up to you two to decide. If I tell the troops, maybe they will think I did it.'

"And the two Navajos talked about it some more. Killing is against the law, and they want the troops to know it was just two Navajo men who did the killing. Then the troops will hunt them down, not blame all the Navajos for the killing.

"So they decided to go to Fort Wingate. But on the way they met the troops from the fort. There were Navajos with them who saw the first killing. The two Navajos and the Mexican told the troops all about the second killing, and they all went to where the first body was buried and took the body out and put it on a mule. And they went to this other place and dug the second body out. They put it on another mule.

"Then they told the two Navajos and the Mexican to stay there overnight, and the next morning they would go with them to find the killers. So everybody made camp, and two or three of the troops took the bodies back to Fort Wingate and buried them over there."

This is the story we are told. Then the troops send a Navajo man to go all around and tell all the Navajo people that the troops are hunting the killers. But somehow the Navajo man don't tell it right, and the Navajo people misunderstand, and some of them start moving to the mountains. They think another war is started. They move with their sheep, horses, cattle. You can see the dust going up from where they are chasing their flocks.

All around us at Thief Rock, where we are growing our crops, there are lots of families moving to the mountains or into the valleys. Nobody knows for sure what is going on. Some are saying, "Another war is starting. Run for your life to the mountain."

There are a whole bunch of people in one place. That man that I told you about from Navajo Mountain, Wounded-Knee, this brave man tells the people that are moving, "Stay where

A warrior with rifle and saddle stands in front of a rock hogan and attached shade shelter. Rifles were rare among the Navajo prior to the Long Walk.

you are." He tells them, "We men can ride to the troops." He
tells the men to come and join him and go to the troops and
ask them some questions. He says, "The troops don't come to
chase us people for no reason at all."

Some of the men agree to go with him. I want to go. I don't
think the treaty is already broken again. I believe the treaty is
signed forever. There are fifty of us, just single men. The married men don't want to go. They think they will get killed. So
those of us that want to go, we get our horses and saddle them.

We ride quite a ways toward Black Mountain. We pass all
these places, and soon we see a whole bunch of troops coming
toward us. We stop on a hill. The troops are down in the wash.
When they see us, they start running around, talking to each
other. Then all of them line up their horses.

We are just wondering what it means when they line up like
that. None of us know what they are going to do. We don't line
up, just stay in a bunch. Then Wounded-Knee calls on about
seven of us to ride over there with him and meet them halfway. We do this. Then eight soldiers do the same—meet us
halfway—and when they stop, they line up their horses just
like the others. And there is a Navajo interpreter with them.
But those Navajo men that told the troops about the killings,
they are staying back with the rest of the troops.

The headman and the Navajo interpreter get off their horses.
So does Wounded-Knee. They shake hands, but Wounded-Knee
says to the headman, "I don't want a fingertip handshake.
Shake my hand like you really mean something." So they hold
hands for a while.[9]

Then they let go of their hands, and Wounded-Knee says,
"That is what I call a friendship way of shaking hands." He
tells us to get down from our horses and shake hands with the

9. In the Navajo way, it is the pressure of the thumb on the back of the
hand and the duration of the clasp that indicates sincerity in the meeting.

headman too. And the headman tells his soldiers to do the same thing.

After that we all sit down, and the headman tells us why they are riding this far. They are looking for those two Navajo men who killed the two white men. The headman says he has two Navajo witnesses who saw it. None of us are sure about the killing, so Wounded-Knee starts questioning the interpreter, asks him if it is Truth. He said it is Truth. The witnesses had named both of them.

The interpreter said, "The first killer was last seen with some Paiutes." He said, "The witnesses think he went back with them to Paiute Canyon." Then he said, "The other killer was last seen with the Mexicans. If he went back with them to Mexico, there's no way we'll find him."

Then the headman asks us if we will go help the soldiers track the killers down. We all said, "No, we don't want to help them, because we don't want any of our people to get killed." And we talk among ourselves, and what we are saying Wounded-Knee tells the Navajo interpreter. He says, "Those two men are dangerous. They got guns, and both of them got lots of friends to help them.

"We Navajos are all living in peace. Lots of us survived the Fort Sumner Long Walk. We want to stay peaceful and raise our children and livestock. We wish to live long and enjoy our land and our lives. We have suffered enough for all these years. Now we are trying hard to live in peace. We don't want any trouble with any other tribe. We think your troops want the same too. They don't want to get killed and they want to live long. So please leave our people alone. But if you find these two men, they are all yours. They are guilty of the killing, and you have witnesses too. And by running away, they show their guilt."

And Wounded-Knee says, "I'm going to take my men back. And I'm going to take the witnesses too. If you keep them

The 1874 Navajo delegation to Washington, D.C. Chief Manuelito and his wife, Juanita, are seated in the center.

Footracing was a traditional source of entertainment at local gatherings.

here, there will be new kinds of troubles started. I don't want that to happen. Lots of people are already afraid. Lots of people have already gone to the mountains. They are afraid the war is started again."

Then the white headman says, "I want you all to move back to where you are living. We are not after you. I know you are living in peace. We are just after those two men, not any of you. Please understand that. We are your friends, and we won't harm you. We shook hands, and it will be like that from now on. And don't be afraid to ask me if you need anything, like a doctor or some food or clothing." After he is through talking, he shakes hands with us again.

All the time that this is going on I don't feel like friends to the troops. What happened before with our people, I am thinking about it. And it makes me really mad. I see all those troops out here just because two white men die. And now they say it's against the law to kill. Where was that law when they were killing all the Navajo people? Thousands of them, shooting them and starving them and letting them walk three hundred miles to a land that isn't theirs, treating them like animals. And here the troops are saying, "We're friends from now on." I don't think they have the right to say that right in front of us. They think the killing of our people is nothing. We have hearts to feel sorry for all our people that got killed, cry for them, miss them all our lives, as long as we live. But I just hold my temper. I just shake their hand, but I know I won't be their friend.

We go back to where the families are gathered for the night. We talk all night with them, tell them what the headman said and what the interpreter said. The interpreter said he had been staying with the troops ever since our people came back from Hwéeldi. He said they are kind.

The next morning the people move back to their hogans and take all their livestock back to where our corn is ripe. Here we

Three men with traditional moccasins, blankets, headbands, and silver-studded pouches.

had left in a hurry, left because we thought there was a new war ready to start, left the ripe corn for the crows and coyotes to eat.

I stay around for one more year. I think about these families that stay and hoe the land. They have lots of help with their sons-in-law and daughters-in-law. Finally I realize they don't need my help anymore, and so I move away.

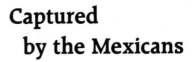

Captured
by the Mexicans

When I leave Thief Rock, I go
here and there to find somebody
that will love me, that cares for me
like my parents did. But I don't really
know what I am looking for. I am an
orphan. I don't have anyone to really
talk to. Before, the warriors were together, and the chief, and we would
talk to each other and help each other
be strong. Now I am alone, and nobody understands how I'm
feeling, or my sorrow.

I know this man. He's my *shinálí*, a clan relative on my
father's side. He's a Tábąąhá (Edgewater Clan). They call him
Chách'osh Nééz, Tall-Syphilis. He tells me I should move in
with his family. He says I'm like his son. He gives me horses
and sheep for my own, but I don't feel like they belong to me.

One day the two of us are riding close by the Hopi village
near Tuba City. We are going west. We got about seven horses
that are our own horses. We are herding them, and we don't
know that we are being followed. We stop north of Shadow
Mountain. We see two Hopi men running on foot after us and
about four Mexican men riding horses behind them. We are
saying, "We thought all the Mexicans are back in their own
land. Here the Hopi are helping Mexicans to catch us, or they
want our horses."

We know there is a trail behind Shadow Mountain, south of
the mountain. It goes down to the Little Colorado River, and
the trail goes across the river. That is where we are going. So

we hurry up and get to the river, and we cross the river, but we miss the trail that will lead us out of the canyon. We miss it. We can't go on. There's rocks and steep banks and the fast river, and we can't get through.

We just keep trying to find a trail to go up the canyon. My partner leaves his horse and goes farther up the steep canyon on foot. He is way up there, just sitting there. But I stay with the horses, still trying to find the trail. That's when the Hopi men catch up with me. They get our horses. The Hopi men catch me too. I think they are going to kill me, but they say, "Let's go."

So the Mexicans take me and eight horses—the seven horses we are herding and my partner's horse too. The Hopi men just jump on my partner's horse and we all take off. The Mexicans finally find the trail we had been looking for. We go east toward Cameron, then after that southeast of Flagstaff. They let the Hopi men go home from there.

I ride with the Mexicans to Mexico. In about five days we get to their land. There are some Navajos already over there. They are kept in a fence. I see them off in the distance, too far away to talk to them. We have our own guard. There is a Navajo boy there too. We stay together and in one place for two years. After a while we understand the Spanish language, and we can talk with them. There is one white man too. After a while we understand him too. We work with him, hunt for horses. They still guard us.

That boy that is there already knows how to ride horses. He is thirteen years old. He was captured while he was herding sheep. He catches on real quick. He can speak English and Spanish. I am lucky I have an interpreter. We sometimes sit around the fire and laugh with the Mexicans. They are our friends. They don't seem like our enemy.

We look at all the Mexican families. They always have a Navajo man or lady or a girl or boy to every Mexican family around them. The family we stay with, there is an old Mexican lady who cooks for us. Our guard has a wife and two kids. I think those Navajos are kept there to be their slaves. They don't let us go near; we just see them in the distance. We don't know how they've been treated.

The family we are staying with is a nice family. They feed us good. One night when we are sitting around, our guard asks us if we want to go home. We think he is just kidding us, so we all joke around. He asks us again, and we both say, "Yes, we want to go home!" The family wants us to leave in the night. They don't want anybody to know they let us go. They give us two horses and some food to take with us. Somebody is taking care of the horses for us about three miles away from where we have been kept. We have to run over there. First the guard shows us the place the horses will be waiting in the daytime. And he makes us a map, how we could go from here to our homeland. He shows us, and the boy really understands how to read the map good. In the night we start running over there. We get over there. Somebody is there taking care of the horses. We just say gracias and adiós to them.

We ride all night and all day. We get to this mountain. We ride up the mountain a little ways and let the horses rest, and we stay there till dawn. We start again after dawn. We ride all night, follow our map. We get to another mountain and rest again. The horses know they are taking us home. They are fat and healthy. We don't even look for water. The horses can smell the water. We go there. We let them drink and rest there again.

In five days' riding we see San Francisco Peaks to our west, and we come up near what we call Béésh Sinil.[10] We rest there again for a day. That is where our map ends.

10. Winslow, Arizona, where the railroad went through.

So we start off on our own. We go toward Albuquerque. We are trying to find the guy that was with me when I was captured. We go on the mesa. We just go slow and let the horses walk. We come up on the west of Mount Taylor to a place where a Navajo lives. We ask for that man that I was with when I was captured. They tell us he lives a mile away from there, so we start again.

When we get to his hogan, the family stops us. They tell us to take the clothes off that we have on, take them off outside. We do it. They already have a ceremony going on for us. I think he already knew we were coming. The medicine man is sitting there, and we wash ourselves with yucca soap. And we put on new clothes. They sing all night. It is a good feeling to come home like that. Tall-Syphilis says, "I'm praying for you all this time." We sit there all night, he asking us questions and we telling them what happened and what we were doing all these two years. We said, "We did have fun. We didn't come to be a slave."

After that, we have to hunt the boy's family. We find them. They say, "We're Honáágháahnii [One-Walks-Around Clan]." The boy was only thirteen when he was captured. Now he is fifteen. They thought he was killed. He was captured when he was herding sheep, and the sheep's the only one that came home. They can't find him. They look all over the place for a year. They finally say, "He's killed somewhere, not alive." They've been crying for him all this time, but finally he came home, so everybody is very happy to see him. We tell the family about what had been happening for two years, and that the Mexicans call me Hombre and the boy, Muchacho. Those were our names for two years. We tell them about the ceremony we both just had too.

When I am leaving, the boy wants to come with me, not stay with his family. He says to me, "I love you. And you teach me lots of things. And I think of you like my father. You're a nice man, and I can't leave you, and you can't leave me," and all those things like that. He wants to go with me.

So I have to sit down and talk with him. "That's the way I think of you too. But I have to leave you here with your family. You helped me a lot, like my own son. And you led me back over here. I don't know why we got together over there. And I think we just have to remember each other like that, because your family wants you here.

"I haven't been married yet," I tell him, "and I don't have a family. I'm just staying with my father's clan relatives over there. So I can't take you with me. So it's good for you to stay here with your family. Your father's here, and your mom and your sister and everybody. So I'll come back and see you sometime. I love you and I'd like to have you stay with me, but I can't take you away from your family. If we hadn't met in Mexico, you'd still be there, not home with your family. But we both helped each other to come home to our homeland. You were captured and supposed to be a slave. But they let us go because of the prayer of our families. You'll be brave as long as you live."

So I leave him, and about a year later I go back over there to see him, because I promised him. It's too far to ride, but I promised. So I go over and see him. The boy is okay then. He is sixteen. He is still the same and really proud of himself. He just says to me, "I sure did miss you for a while. I'm okay, and I got used to my family again. And I'm glad you talk to me like that. It's still in my mind what you told me. I still remember that." That's what he says. "I still love you," he says. And he says, "My grandmother wants me to get married. She says I'm old enough, but I'm not. I'm only sixteen." He asks me if it's okay if he gets married when he's only sixteen. I tell him, "It's up to you. You just have to think about it more. If you have a family, you have to be working for them, not yourself. So think about it some more." That's what I say to him.

A shade shelter of cedar posts and brush keeps out the harsh summer sun but admits cool breezes. Here meat is drying and water has been hauled in for a special occasion.

So he butchers a sheep and makes me a feast with him, and puts some on the horse with me. And I just promise him, "Maybe someday I'll come and see you again." The next year, when he is seventeen, I get word from him to come to his wedding. But I can't go. I live too many days' trip to the west.

Even after lots of years I think of him, how smart he was when I met him. I am older than him, but he is smarter than me. Just a young boy, and I'm really proud of him, like he was my own son.

Making a Living

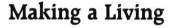

I don't have a wife, and
there are just a few
women and girls—the
ones that come back from
Hwéeldi. A year after I come
back from my capture in Mexico, I marry a woman near Kay-
enta. She is a Kinyaa'áanii [The-Towering-House Clan]. After I
get five kids, I move my family to the west, near Dinnehotso.
My wife gets sick and dies a year later.

I move in with all my in-laws, and the grandma takes care
of all the kids. A year later the grandma tells me to marry my
first wife's younger sister. I do, and she starts taking care of the
kids. She and I get four more kids.

The first five grow up, and they are married. We get grandchildren. And again, my second wife dies.

Our children all grow up, and one of my daughters dies. She
has two little girls, my grandkids. I take them with me. I decide to go to Navajo Mountain. I know that area well. That's
where I lived with my warriors for four years, guarding our
people while the rest of our people were at Hwéeldi. I know
where there is water, and I know where there is good feed for
livestock. We go where I used to go.

I don't know why these people that went to Hwéeldi, they
still don't want to talk about it—what happened there. I want
to talk about my tragic story, because if I don't, it will get into
my mind and get into my dream and make me crazy. I know
some people died of their tragic story. They think about it and
think about how many relatives they lost. Their parents got
shot. They get into shock. That is what kills them. That is

why we warriors have to talk to each other. We wake ourselves up, get out of the shock. And that is why I tell my kids what happened, so it won't be forgot.

So at Navajo Mountain I show my children around. I show them where the Navajos stayed, hiding in the canyon, planting corn, watermelon, and peaches for the people to survive. I show my children around, and they tell me, "You were a brave man." They know Navajo Mountain is a big mountain. They look up to the mountain. I take them where I used to go. People already live here and there. The good places are already taken. We camp close to where there is water and near where some of my relatives live. We live here for a year. There is another kind of suffering I get into, like loneliness. I miss my children's mom.

Navajo Mountain is where I meet another girl. She is twenty-five years old. She is half my age. I marry her. She raises my two granddaughters. She is Bịịh Bitoodnii (Deer-Spring Clan).

Even though I am older than her, she just marries me. She is a kind lady. She loves us—me and my grandchildren. She is living with her relatives, and they're all a kind family. Her father is a medicine man, and the family has lots of sheep and goats.

When we get married and move, her family gives us a whole bunch of sheep and goats to make a living. They give us horses, too, so we can move. Her mother has already taught her how to weave. That's the only thing we support ourselves with when we start living together. She weaves big rugs and is a fast weaver.

We move toward Tuba City to find a place where I can plant some corn. We finally settle at Kerley Valley. I fix a place to plant corn and cantaloupe and peach trees, and we have some sheep and horses. We move them to Shadow Mountain.

I still am with my children. We all move there. They are all married and have kids, and they have sheep and cattle. They

*Teamwork is important to survival in the desert. Here men join to-
gether to cut, haul, and erect the timbers for a Navajo structure.*

have a good living. They have everything they need—wagons too. They all live close by, and I see them every day. And the two granddaughters grow up and get married too.

The first two kids that I have with this lady die. Then we get a son who lives. The next two kids die. There was nothing wrong with the kids that die. Just grow to two years old, then die.

Finally we get another son, ten years later. After that we get two girls and two sons.[11] We have five on Deer-Spring Clan. Soon I am a great-great-grandfather by my oldest children.

Soon after I get to Kerley Valley, I work for the government by doing Pony Express. I carry mail from Tuba City to Flagstaff and bring the new mail back. I just use my own horses. I get paid two dollars when I get back with the mail—and a hundred-pound sack of flour.

If we have lots of mail, like boxes, my son and grandson and two or three others take the wagon. There are about six wagons that go to Flagstaff to get mail and some supplies for the school. The wagons each have six horses. Still it is hard to pull the wagon in the snow. Snow won't come off metal wagon wheels. It just gets frozen on. You have to get off and walk by the wheel and hit it as it's going along. In the winter we all have a hard time coming back from Flagstaff. If there's a lot of snow, we just sleep over there by Sacred Mountain Store. Two old men own the store and let the men who carry Pony Express on horse or wagon sleep there. The wagons have to go on the road, but me and my horse can go on the horse trail, which is shorter than the road.

After that we quit hauling mail. We start to get coal from the coal mine southeast of Tuba City. We haul the coal for the school to keep it warm and for the powerhouse. There's six horses to each wagon, and four men. This is a worse job than the mail. The distance is a little shorter than to Flagstaff, but

11. Tiana Bighorse is his oldest daughter of the Deer Spring Clan.

it is too hard work. There are about twenty Navajo wagons
that go over there, and Hopis go too. They have about ten wagons of their own. We have to get in line with the wagons to get
a load. Sometimes you have to stay overnight, waiting to load.
Sometimes it takes three days to go get a load and bring it
back. We just use our shovel to get a load. If men know each
other, or are in the same family, they don't just fill their wagons and go. They have to stay and help the ones they know. So
if there are four wagons, the men load together and leave at the
same time.

When it is snowing it is really too hard and cold. We suffer cold and hunger going over there and coming back. For all
four of us, we just get a sack of one hundred pounds of flour
and a bale of hay for our horses. And twenty-five dollars a
wagonload.

Every time I come home there's about twenty families waiting for me. Everybody has a bowl and wants some flour. They
always get it. Nobody is turned down.

Various tribes often convened to bargain and trade wares on pueblo feast days.

Indian education was required by the treaty of 1868. Boarding schools like this one at Keams Canyon were designed to fit the white man's geometric sensibility.

How I Got the Name Bighorse

As I told you, my wife is a fast weaver. She makes saddle blankets and big rugs. I take them to Utah to trade them for some horses. I go to Tropic, Utah. That is what they call a mountain that has a white face. I get one big stallion and two female horses with two little female ponies. I get those horses from a Mormon family. There are four Navajo men that go over there with me. They all get horses the same as I got, but no stallion. I'm the only one that gets a big stallion.

All the females get ponies and grow big, so after two years I got lots of horses. They're all big ones. The Navajo horses are all smaller than mine. I always have somebody to tame the horses for me. I always give them a horse to pay them, so there is always somebody who wants to tame them for me.

Pretty soon I got lots of horses. I never count them. I always have an extra horse to ride. All my in-laws have horses from me. The men that came with me and got horses didn't get a big stallion to breed their female horses with, so they don't have big horses. I'm the only one. That is how I got my name,

Biłį́į́'ntsaazii, Bighorse. I'm proud of my name. I think I'm the only one whose name is Bighorse.

Horses were my companion all my life. They are kind to me and save my life. When the Mexicans were chasing me, the horses ran for their lives. The Mexicans were good shooters. While I was laying on one of the horses, the bullet hit me. But somehow it went under my skin and stopped there. The bullet didn't go any farther. It is because of the horses. They kept running fast. They still kept running after I jumped down. Two days later I found them, and they were all happy to see me. They started running to me. I met them. They all stood around me and wanted to be pet on their nose.

At that time the horses know what to do. They don't want to let their rider get shot. They don't want to get shot themselves. They know how to hide, even behind a little tree. They can stand still. They can hide their voice and their foot noise.

When you talk to them, they will listen. They know the enemy is around. They can stand still in one place for a long time, till the rider comes back.

Some Navajo men know a song for the horse and have a sacred name for the horse. It makes supernatural powers that can make a horse stay stronger and go as far as his master goes without water. This horse's name goes on generation after generation. It is a secret. They keep it in the family.

The sheep are like that too. When you take care of them, herd them around, they know you and know your voice. They know where the corral is and know what time they come home. The rams and billy goats take care of them. They know how to fight coyotes.

You have to herd the sheep every day. You have to be there for them all the time, bring them back to the corral. Sometimes you bring them back at noon. That is in the summertime, and the day is longer. In the winter the day is short, and you don't herd them all day. When they have lambs, you don't

herd them with the sheep. The lambs have to stay in the corral, so you have to bring the sheep home earlier because the
little lambs get so hungry. It's fun to have lots of pet lambs.
They know you and can't wait to get fed. And you have to
bring the sheep home when it is still daylight so they know
which are their lambs. If you bring them back too late, when
it's dark, the sheep can't find *their* lambs. They will be crying
and smelling all around, but they can't find the right one.

The Horse Race

One time I go to a horse race. They don't have a rodeo like calf-roping or riding a bull or riding horses that buck. They have a horse race. Sometimes they see who can saddle the horse fastest, or they have a chicken pull. In the chicken pull, there's a sack in the ground with money in it, and you have to reach down while your horse is running to get that sack out. Everybody's horse is running around in a circle around the sack. Everyone is trying to get it at the same time. When you get it out, you have to run because everyone will ride their horse after you, chase you. You have to have a fast horse and be strong so they won't take the money away from you.

Sometimes they see who can saddle the horse fastest, but this time they decide to do something different. They say, "Who will light a tobacco fast while riding a horse?" There are five men who want to try it. I say, "I'll join you." And I never have smoked in my life.

At this time they have a little bag of tobacco from the store and some papers to roll it in. It's hard to roll it when you are just standing there.

They have a horse already tame and four years old. Whoever wins the race is going to get the tame horse. They tell us to roll the tobacco and light it while we are on our own horse and the horse is running. They tell us, "Don't stop."

We get everything ready. I say to my horse, "Don't stop till we get to the finish line." I just tie the reins together and put them on the saddle horn to keep them out of my hand.

I try it. My horse is fast and I win! The tame horse is mine! I am surprised I did it so fast, in such a short distance. I like the tobacco; it's the first time I've tasted it. But I never smoke again.

Horses belong to the men and are celebrated in Navajo legend, song, and prayer. The ability to communicate with the horse, to urge it to greater speed and stamina, is a source of pride among men.

The trading post is a place to socialize, hear what's going on, and re-plenish supplies. Here a group of men sit around eating canned goods and perhaps gambling.

More Raiding

There is plenty of rain and plenty of grass in these days. You can't even see the ground. It is covered with tall grasses and sunflowers and *azee' ntł'iní.*[12] You can only see the back of the sheep when they are in it.

More than fifty years before, when the people came back from Hwéeldi, some were given sheep and goats, just two or three to a family. Some got them at Fort Defiance, some at Fort Sumner.

Before they went to Hwéeldi the people had lots of sheep, thousands and thousands—maybe eight thousand. But after Hwéeldi there was just a few left. And ever since they came back, the people had been praying to the Holy People to bless them with all kinds of livestock—for sheep and goats and horses and water and for grazing land, and for all these things to increase. The hope and prayers of our people were answered, and now there are animals all over the reservation and lots of grass.

The government don't like it. They say the feed is not enough, and they say too many animals will ruin the land. They want the Navajo to get rid of their livestock. The Navajo

12. Glovemallow.

don't have a place to sell their goats or sheep or horses, so the government just sends some workers to the reservation. They shoot lots of horses and take lots of goats,[13] all kinds of goats—the blue,[14] the black, the brown, the white.

We Navajo think the government broke the treaty again. They told us to put our weapons down, and here they are shooting all our livestock—the only food we live on. Some of the Navajos try to stop them by taking their herds and hiding them somewhere in a canyon. The policemen and the government workers just go all around and find them. And they pick the people up and put them in jail in Fort Defiance, even the ladies.

The people are angry. They just say, "Go ahead and put us in jail again. Let us starve again." They say, "You got all our food again." We just think that the government is planning another Long Walk for us.

It is heartbreak for me when they do that. I had lots of horses, and the tame ones are the only ones they leave me. Out of two hundred, it is just twenty-five left to about six families. Only four horses to every family. Not even enough. Some are used for the wagon, some horses for the races, some for carrying mail to Flagstaff.

I lose so many. They just get shot. I have to cry for them. I love them all. They were big, beautiful horses. I miss them all my life.

I feel this is the end of my name, Bighorse. And my life. I can't live without my horses. But my kids just tell me my name is still my name and that I am fortunate to have those horses all my life. Now I am old, they tell me, so just let them go.

---

13. For a summary of the government stock reduction program, see the Historical Context entry for 1933–1945.

14. Grey.

My Last Journey

I'm old, but inside I'm strong. I'm blind, but I still want to do all the things I always did. I don't want to just lay here and wait to die. I want to go around and visit my grandchildren, not just stay in one place.

I send word to my children, and someone always brings me a horse to ride over there. I go to their hogan, just for a few days. And then I go again, to another place. I have lots of grandchildren. Everybody wants me to stay, but I don't want to. I just want to keep going.

I know old men like me. People have to take them out to pee. But I don't want people to do that for me. So I just tell my wife to spin me a long, thick wool rope and braid three pieces together to make it strong. And I tell my kids to tie it to the hogan doorpost. Then I say, "Go out and dig a hole behind a bush somewhere, and put a post there. Then," I say, "tie the end of the rope to the post." Then I can just hold onto the rope and walk to its end by myself. When I'm finished, they can take that post out and put it behind the bushes again somewhere else.

Sometimes I have a dream about a man with white hair and a white beard, and his gown is white. Everything about him is white. And he comes to me and says, "I will come again, when your hair will be as white as me."

He comes to me once in a while, not all the time. I always think I'm not ready yet. Sometimes I think he is the one guiding me all my life—saves me, and now he doesn't want me to suffer. He wants me to go where I won't ever suffer from old age.

This man comes to me and says there are old people that come to the end of their journey, and they're living someplace else. And they are kind to everybody that comes to that place.

I think there's another world for these old people. He wants me to go there, so I'll be going over there, and that will be my last journey.

Historical Context

The Navajo is the largest Indian tribe in the United States, with a population of more than 200,000. They live on reservations totaling more than 16 million acres in Arizona, New Mexico, and Utah, and have traditionally been a rural people who have sustained themselves through sheepherding, weaving, and agriculture. As such, they do not live clustered in tight villages—but rather, spread out over the land. They are matrilineal, with individuals tracing blood relationships through their mothers and remaining lifelong members of their mother's clan. The following is a chronology of significant events in Navajo and American history and in the life of Gus Bighorse.

1200S	SEVERE DROUGHT conditions in the Southwest. Some large Anasazi Indian communities are abandoned.
1300S	THE NAVAJO AND APACHE ARRIVE from the north.
1492	COLUMBUS sails to the West Indies.
1519	CORTÉS conquers Mexico and establishes New Spain.
1519– 1800	EXTREME DEPOPULATION of Central and North American Indians due to smallpox, diphtheria, and other Old World diseases brought by Spanish and English settlers.
1540	CORONADO explores New Mexico.
1598	OÑATE colonizes New Mexico, introducing sheep and horses. Approximately 10 million Indians live in North America.
1607	JAMESTOWN is established as the first permanent English settlement in the New World.
1610	SANTA FE is established as the capital of New Mexico.
1610– 1680	SPANISH CATHOLIC MISSIONARY WORK among the Pueblo Indians is extensive.
1620	PILGRIMS land at Plymouth Rock.

1680   PUEBLO REVOLT. Pueblo Indians unite against the in-
        vading, Christianizing Spaniards, killing 400 and caus-
        ing the rest, numbering about 1,950, to retreat.
        The non-native population on the North American
        continent is approximately 155,000.

1692   VARGAS reconquers New Mexico for Spain. He se-
        verely chastises Indian groups, destroys several vil-
        lages, and enters Santa Fe. Indians occupying the capi-
        tal yield peacefully. Later, Vargas suppresses Pueblo
        rebellions, and many Pueblo Indians flee to the Navajo
        country for protection.

1763   ENGLAND claims almost all land between the Atlantic
        Ocean and the Mississippi River.

1775   THE FIRST CONTINENTAL CONGRESS establishes Depart-
        ments of Indian Affairs to serve the English colonies.
        Two of the commissioners are Benjamin Franklin and
        Patrick Henry.

1776   NARBONA is born. He becomes a Navajo leader who
        works for peace, but he is killed by U.S. troops in
        1849.
        DECLARATION OF INDEPENDENCE.

1781–   Under the ARTICLES OF CONFEDERATION, Indians have
1789   special areas to hunt and live on but cannot dispose of
        land without the consent of the U.S. government. As a
        result of the war between Britain and the American
        colonies in 1783, the United States claims all land for-
        merly held by England.

1787   THE NORTHWEST ORDINANCE, passed by Congress,
        states that the United States will not take Indians'
        land without their consent; that the land will not be
        invaded or disturbed unless in wars authorized by
        Congress; that the United States will enact laws
        founded in justice and humanity to preserve peace and
        friendship with the Indians; and that Indians are not
        citizens and will be neither taxed nor represented in
        Congress.

1800– TREATIES OF CESSION. The United States obtains mil-
1871   lions of acres of Indian land for the purpose of remov-
       ing Indians from the path of westward migration.

1803   THE LOUISIANA PURCHASE. After buying additional land
       from France, President Thomas Jefferson claims terri-
       tory all the way to the Rio Grande and so challenges
       Spanish land claims.

1819   MANUELITO is born. As a headman of the Navajo, he is
       called Angry-Warrior because he prefers war talk to
       peace talk and openly disagrees with Narbona's work
       for peace.

1821– MEXICAN PERIOD. Mexico becomes independent of
1846   Spain, and New Mexico becomes a province of Mex-
       ico. Indians, as citizens of Mexico, are equals of non-
       Indians.

1822   THE SANTA FE TRAIL is opened for trade with the
       United States, and goods begin to flow across the
       plains from the east.

1824   THE BUREAU OF INDIAN AFFAIRS is established by the
       United States under the Department of War.

1829   ANDREW JACKSON, renowned in the Southeast as an In-
       dian fighter, becomes president of the United States
       and is later reelected.

1830   THE INDIAN REMOVAL ACT. The United States moves
       Indians to lands west of the Mississippi in exchange
       for their lands east of the river.

1844   JAMES K. POLK runs for president of the United States
       on a Manifest Destiny platform favoring expansion
       westward and calling for the acquisition of California,
       Oregon, and Texas.

Gus Bighorse is born about this time.

1846   THE MEXICAN-AMERICAN WAR. General Stephen W.
       Kearny acquires New Mexico for the United States.
       The U.S. military stays to "keep the peace" between
       Indians and settlers.

1848– Through the TREATY OF GUADALUPE-HIDALGO of 1848
1853   and the Gadsden Purchase of 1853, the United States
       gains sovereignty over most of the southwestern por-
       tion of the present-day United States and jurisdiction
       over many thousands of Indians living there. The
       treaty states that all Mexican citizens can become
       citizens of the United States, but subsequent U.S.
       court decisions often deny Indians citizenship rights.

1849   THE BUREAU OF INDIAN AFFAIRS is transferred to the
       newly created Department of the Interior. BIA policies
       favor limiting Indians to subsistence by agriculture
       rather than hunting to make more land available for
       white settlers.
       The first Indian agent in New Mexico, James S. Cal-
       houn, is appointed.

1854   PUEBLO LAND GRANTS receive confirmation by the U.S.
       government but no protection, as Indians are still not
       considered U.S. citizens.

*Gus Bighorse, from age nine to age thirteen, rides the Navajo
lands with his father.*

1860   ABRAHAM LINCOLN is elected president, and seven
       southern states soon secede from the Union.

1861   THE CIVIL WAR begins.

1862   SOUTHERN OFFICERS leave New Mexico to fight for the
       Confederacy. Troops are redeployed to oppose a Con-
       federate invasion rather than control Indian tribes.
       The Confederate invasion is halted near Santa Fe.
       GENERAL JAMES CARLETON arrives with his California
       Column too late to fight Confederate forces. He be-
       comes commander of the Department of New Mexico
       and forms new Indian policy. He warns Indian leaders
       that all who do not "respect the peace" will be pun-
       ished, and he sends troops against Indians who "con-
       tinue to raid." KIT CARSON is given orders to defeat the

Indians, not to bargain with them. He destroys Navajo
livestock and crops and kills those who won't submit.

*Gus Bighorse's parents are killed. He goes to the mountains
and joins others. At about age sixteen he becomes a leader of
several bands of warriors.*

1864– THE LONG WALK. General Carleton orders defeated
1868   Navajos at Fort Defiance (Arizona) to be placed on res-
       ervations to learn Christianity and farming. They are
       force-marched 325 miles to Fort Sumner on the Pecos
       River (eastern New Mexico). There, within an area
       known as Bosque Redondo, the captured Navajos are
       incarcerated along with the Mescalero Apache. The
       Navajo and Mescalero Apache do not get along. Plains
       Indians raid Bosque Redondo. Crops fail. The land will
       not support the population of 9,000. Food, fuel, and
       clothing are in short supply. The United States finds
       reservations costly to operate.

*Gus Bighorse goes behind Navajo Mountain to help protect
the thousands of Navajos who haven't been caught.*

1865   THE MESCALERO APACHES are permitted to leave
       Bosque Redondo and return to the Fort Stanton area.

1868   THE TREATY OF BOSQUE REDONDO. General William T.
       Sherman lets the Navajo return home if they agree
       never to fight again. The treaty (1) provides for a reser-
       vation of about 3.5 million acres, one-tenth of the land
       the Navajo previously needed to support themselves;
       (2) compels Navajo children to attend reservation
       schools, the first of which is built in 1883, though not
       until 1950 are enough schools built to accommodate
       even half the children; and (3) promises to give the
       Navajo 15,000 sheep, which arrive one and a half years
       later; 500 cattle; and rations, which turn out to be
       meager and irregular.

1869   ACT OF 1869. Congress settles the remaining Indians on reservations and appoints a Board of Indian Commissioners, which contracts with major religious denominations to operate reservation schools.

1870   THE NAVAJO POPULATION is about 9,000, with 30,000 sheep. By 1880 the population is about 16,000, with 700,000 sheep.

Gus Bighorse is captured by Mexicans and taken to Mexico.

1871   THE INDIAN APPROPRIATION ACT forbids future Indian treaties. In the ninety-three years since 1778, almost 400 treaties have been negotiated between Congress and Indian tribes. By them, Indians have ceded about 1 billion acres to the United States, receiving in return inalienable and tax-exempt lands, and in some cases promises of medical care, education, rations, or other things.

Gus Bighorse marries a woman of the Kinyaa'áanii Clan and by her has five children. When she dies, he marries her sister and has four children by her.

1876   THE BATTLE OF THE LITTLE BIG HORN. Sitting Bull's Sioux Indians defeat Gen. George Custer and the Seventh Cavalry.

1878–   LAND ADDITIONS. By 1878 the Navajo reservation, es-
1884   tablished by the treaty of 1868, is overcrowded and overgrazed. Approximately 8,000 Navajos are living outside its boundaries. Between 1878 and 1884 the United States adds to the reservation, increasing its size to over 8 million acres.

1881   TRAINS begin passing through Navajo country, bringing liquor and other outside goods.

1886   THE UNITED STATES USES NAVAJO TROOPS to quell constantly raiding Apaches under Geronimo. This ends the last major Indian war. The Chiricahua Apaches are exiled to Florida. Twenty-seven years later they are

permitted to return to the Southwest to live on the
Mescalero Apache Reservation (New Mexico).

1892 THE COMPULSORY INDIAN EDUCATION ACT is passed
by Congress. Eight boarding schools are built on the
Navajo reservation, one at Tuba City. The Navajo re-
tain children at home to perpetuate traditional activities such as sheepherding and weaving until police accompany agents to force children to attend schools.
Mining companies become interested in a strip of land
given to the Navajo in 1884. President Benjamin Har-
rison orders "all Navajo lands lying west of 100 degrees west longitude and within the Territory of Utah"
restored to the public domain.

*Gus Bighorse moves to Navajo Mountain. When he is fifty, he
marries Tiana's mother. They move to Tuba City. Over the
next twenty-five years, they have five children and he hauls
coal for the Tuba City Boarding School.*

1901 THEODORE ROOSEVELT becomes president.

1912 NEW MEXICO AND ARIZONA are admitted to the Union.

Tiana Bighorse is born.

1917 DURING WORLD WAR I, the United States declares war
on Germany and Austria-Hungary.

1923 THE NAVAJO TRIBAL COUNCIL is established.

1924 ALL INDIANS ARE GRANTED CITIZENSHIP.

1928 THE MERRIAM REPORT, which reveals the shocking social and economic conditions of American Indians,
leads to the Indian Reorganization Act of 1934.

*Gus Bighorse is about eighty-two and blind. His youngest
son, Floyd, who is seven, cares for him.*

1932 FRANKLIN DELANO ROOSEVELT is elected president. Additional land is given to the Navajo, bringing the reservation to 16 million acres.

1933–   JOHN COLLIER serves as commissioner of Indian affairs.
1945   Collier and government experts determine that Navajo
land is overgrazed and institute a mandatory livestock
reduction program. They insist that a proportion of all
horses, cows, sheep, and goats be destroyed. But as the
entire life of the Navajo revolves around their livestock, the Navajo refuse. Government agents shoot
thousands of animals. Many rot in place; some are
piled and burned. Collier is remembered by the Navajo
as a second Kit Carson.

Gus Bighorse's horses are shot by government agents.

1934   THE INDIAN REORGANIZATION ACT encourages Indian
groups to reorganize and exercise their sovereignty
through governments based on tribal constitutions
and bylaws.

THE JOHNSON-O'MALLEY ACT enables the BIA to make
contracts with public-school districts to enroll Indian
students.

1935   THE NAVAJO VOTE DOWN A PROPOSED CONSTITUTION in
reaction to Collier's stock reduction program.

1936   FIFTY NEW DAY SCHOOLS are opened on the Navajo
reservation so that children can be educated close to
home.

*Gus Bighorse dies in 1939 after ninety-three winters—maybe
more.*

Index

ILLUSTRATION CREDITS

p. xvi. Photograph by John Running.

pp. 4–5. Photograph by James Mooney, 1892; Smithsonian Institution, National Anthropological Archives.

p. 12. Courtesy Museum of New Mexico, neg. no. 23130.

p. 16. Engraving, courtesy U.S. Army Signal Corps Collections in the Museum of New Mexico, neg. no. 14516.

p. 20. Photograph by Edward S. Curtis, 1906; Smithsonian Institution, National Anthropological Archives.

p. 23. Smithsonian Institution, National Anthropological Archives.

p. 24. Photograph by John K. Hillers, courtesy Museum of New Mexico, neg. no. 122772.

p. 29. Courtesy Museum of New Mexico, neg. no. 58388.

p. 38. Courtesy U.S. Army Signal Corps Collections in the Museum of New Mexico, neg. no. 38191.

p. 39. Courtesy Museum of New Mexico, neg. no. 1816.

p. 48. Photograph by Timothy H. O'Sullivan, courtesy Museum of New Mexico, neg. no. 72631.

pp. 64–65. Photograph by Ben Wittick, courtesy School of American Research Collections in the Museum of New Mexico, neg. no. 16017.

pp. 68–69. Photograph by Charles M. Bell, 1874; Smithsonian Institution, National Anthropological Archives.

p. 70. Photograph by Simeon Schwemberger; Smithsonian Institution, National Anthropological Archives.

p. 72. Photograph by Edward S. Curtis; Smithsonian Institution, National Anthropological Archives.

pp. 78–79. Photograph by G. Wharton James, 1898; Smithsonian Institution, National Anthropological Archives.

p. 83. Photograph by Simeon Schwemberger; Smithsonian Institution, National Anthropological Archives.

pp. 86–87. Photograph by T. Harmon Parkhurst, courtesy Museum of New Mexico, neg. no. 3099.

p. 88. Photograph by Herbert W. Gleason; Smithsonian Institution, National Anthropological Archives.

p. 93. Photograph by Simeon Schwemberger; Smithsonian Institution, National Anthropological Archives.

p. 94. Photograph by Sumner W. Matteson; Smithsonian Institution, National Anthropological Archives.

About the Author

TIANA BIGHORSE, who chooses to use the last name of Bighorse in honor of her father, was born north of Tuba City, Arizona, in 1917 and is a member of the Deer Spring Clan. At the age of seven she began two activities that would become important aspects of her life: she started school at the Tuba City Boarding School and she started to weave. Her school career lasted through the ninth grade, a remarkable achievement for a Navajo of her generation. Her weaving career has lasted more than sixty years. Tiana's mother taught her the skills—and the pride—of weaving, just as she had been taught by her mother before her. Tiana was a contributor to *Halo of the Sun: Stories Told and Retold* and to *The Weaver's Pathway: A Clarification of the "Spirit Trail" in Navajo Weaving.* She is the coauthor with Noël Bennett of *Working with the Wool: How to Weave a Navajo Rug.*

About the Editor

NOËL BENNETT came to the Navajo reservation in 1968 with advanced degrees in art and education from Stanford University. For eight years she immersed herself in Navajo life and Navajo weaving and began a deep and lifelong friendship with Tiana Bighorse. Together they sheared the sheep, collected plants to dye the wool, carded, spun, and wove. Tiana took her into her family.

In the following years, Noël passed these gifts along to others. She gave Navajo weaving workshops, conferences, and lectures across the country; forged Navajo rug restoration techniques; and founded the nonprofit corporation Shared Horizons, of which she is director. Her other books include *Working with the Wool: How to Weave a Navajo Rug; Designing with the Wool: Advanced Techniques in Navajo Weaving; Weaver's Pathway: A Clarification of the "Spirit Trail" in Navajo Weaving;* and *Halo of the Sun: Stories Told and Retold.*

For the last five years, Noël has pursued *A Place in the Wild*, a study of architecture in fragile natural environments. This project is sponsored by Shared Horizons and supported in part by a grant from the National Endowment for the Arts. Noël lives and works in Corrales, New Mexico.